ALIENATION OF DONT'E IZZO

BANGOR MAINE'S
ENDEMIC CLANDESTINE HOMGENEITY

Don and Kelly Izzo

Chapter Art by Dont'e Izzo

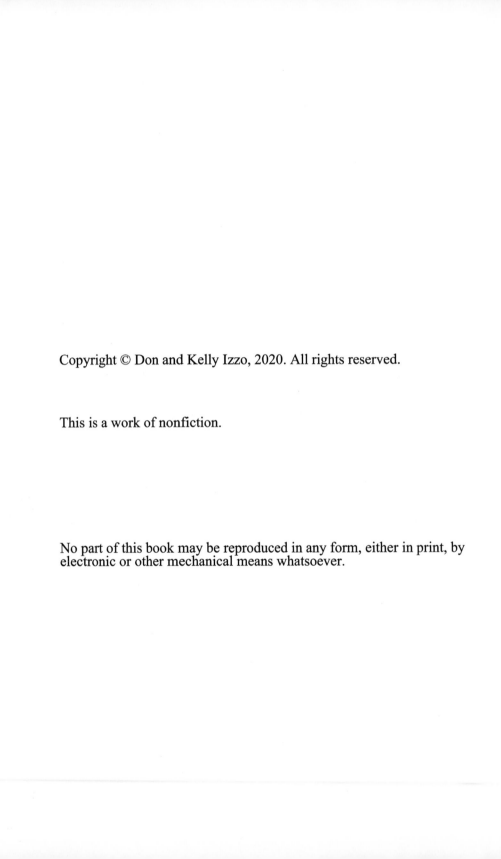

Contents

Definition of

Endemic

Clandestine Homogeneity

A widespread, systematic, covert preference, practiced and encouraged by people of a certain region, in furtherance of sameness in ideology, culture, and perspective, which results in the alienation of others.

Love Is
Eternal

Imagine, in the wake of a tragedy, being at the mercy of individuals and bureaucratic institutions contemptuous of your grief.

Imagine being a lone voice in a sea of indifference, crying out for answers, and receiving hallow responses—or, worse, silence.

Imagine having to bury your child without an ounce of support from cogs in the colossal machine of government. Content to violate the law, they won't advocate for your cause or act on your behalf.

When you seek due process and justice, you're told that your defeat will be a foregone conclusion because a jury of your peers "won't like you."

Imagine being a pawn to the constant shifting of responsibility, only to discover that no one, even at the highest levels of government, will address your inquiries or demonstrate a modicum of empathy— through deeds, not words.

Imagine...but you need not conjure such thoughts in the abstract. This is our story, our truth.

The crusade continues!

Don and Kelly Izzo

PREFACE

Hey, I'm Dont'e Andrew Izzo, and I loved the world. Sound funny? Well, it's true. I loved and got along with everyone—from teachers to peers and schoolmates. I always did what I was told, and I never disobeyed my parents. It's not because I was afraid of them. No! They were cool. They loved and nurtured me like no other parents I knew. By all appearances, I was cheerful, never frowned or was angry, and I absolutely refused to say "S--t." See? It just wasn't me.

I was an all-American kid, ran cross country, played football, and joined the JROTC, hoping to serve my country. I was excited about taking driving lessons, getting my license, and acquiring my dad's truck. I had everything to live for . . .

*But one day, I slipped into the dark night. No one knew why—least of all my parents. I never meant to hurt them, but I had to do it—leave the world, I mean—the world that I loved so much. Things were becoming too hard— the bullying, the coercion from people I thought were my friends who turned me against myself. I saw no way out, but I want everyone—do you hear me world?—**EVERYONE*** *must know that every life has value and it doesn't have to be this way.*

People should be kind to one another, live and let live, no matter what race, gender, culture, or religion they happen to be. All of us have a purpose. I had a purpose—but I didn't know it.

Every human being should also be accountable— especially people in authority tasked with protecting our world's youth. I was betrayed by the very individuals and entities who should have protected me—namely, the United States' premier watchdog for suicide prevention. If only my call were heeded! If only people had reached out, things would have been different. Now, even in death, my voice will not be silenced.

From my vantage point above the fray of indifference, I have a clearer vision of what took place and a mission to prevent similar tragedies and save other lives.

Don't make the same choice that I did. Where there is life, there is hope and a chance to change conditions—and the world. **CHOOSE LIFE**, *seek and demand help, and do as I always did: Listen to my parents, Donald and Kelly Izzo, the guardians of my story.*

If Dont'e were here, we are certain that he would want to convey the foregoing message. As the embodiments of our son's legacy, we are entrusted with carrying the torch of justice in his name and speaking in his voice—not solely to give purpose to a precious life cut short by human and institutional indifference, but to perpetuate the worldview that we infused in him: universal tolerance, love of one's fellow human beings, the beauty of diversity, and the notion of *e pluribus unum* ("out of many, one"), the United States motto, etched in the Great Seal.

That philosophy of inclusiveness and collective consciousness was, somehow, negated in our son's case, and all attempts to seek help—from his high school's staff and administration, from local to state law enforcement, to the highest levels of government—fell on deaf ears.

To turn a cold shoulder signifies complicity in the outcome of any given circumstance, especially when that end result is the death of a child—*our child* who, throughout time, received the love and comfort of an ideal home, a cherub whose smile lit up the universe, a boy who, on home video, hilariously dramatized our journey to the corner store for a hot dog as though it were a suspense thriller.

Complicity, facilitation, conspiracy. We do not use these terms lightly, but where safety, well-being, and life are concerned, those who are wronged must call things as they are. We do not take any pleasure whatsoever in allocating blame, but in an instance in which a precious life is senselessly lost—*our life*, our son—we have no choice but to divulge our truth.

Before Donté's passing, neither of us was versed in social media nor were we aware of the platforms' far-reaching impact —and when used improperly, their destructive nature. Those with a propensity for violence use cyber venues for the most nefarious purposes—such as inferring that a fifteen-year-old boy must know "how to kill himself."

Such criminal mentality, coupled with intention and action, are lethal. Our son was caught in the middle and ultimately lured into an abyss of desperation and despair.

In the aftermath of the tragedy, those charged with his care and protection must be held accountable, and we are mindful that we bear the onus of responsibility to self-reflect and ask "why?" However, as we deliberate and agonize, night and day, the answers elude us.

Dont'e was a 'happy-go-lucky' child, the dearest, sweetest, most enchantingly innocent boy we have ever known—and we do not speak of him only from a subjective parental viewpoint, but as objective observers of his nature. From grammar school to the first quarter of the tenth grade, he maintained a 3.0 grade point average and was universally liked and lauded by teachers and peers alike.

Our home was a haven for boyhood antics, Friday night movies, and games of all types. Our hearts were open to in-depth discussions about life and people, cautionary talks about the fickle, sometimes devious, unexpected behaviors of those we typically trust and hold in high regard; but our big-hearted son could only process our warnings theoretically. When squarely confronted with the cold truth, he could not believe in the mere *possibility* of such conduct— least of all from his friends.

Ultimately, Dont'e was placed under duress, lured, and coerced to witness, experience or participate in *something* so antithetical to his nature that he was unable to live with himself.

His suicide note read, "I'm sorry you had to find this, but I can't take it anymore. No, it's not the grades or what will happen, but it's what kind of edged me off. I love you both, Mom and Dad."

Apparently, the world as our son discovered it to be was filled with betrayal and human failings—a community of individuals who drove him to self-annihilation by relegating him to that society's periphery—to 'otherness,' while others gloated over his devaluation and did absolutely *nothing* to save him.

All the while, he endured in silence, unable to utter the horrible truth—even to us. "Why?" That question belongs to us more than anyone. Perhaps, it was an understandable generation gap, a feeling of uneasiness in divulging information that would, undoubtedly cause distress (that is, he was being victimized by the illusorily powerful, seeking to snuff out his joy, his purpose). Most likely, we will never know the real reason. Nonetheless, we can memorialize his legacy of love and goodwill for humanity. At the same time, we hope to raise awareness regarding institutional and human indifference to the plight of youth who slip the bonds of earth because one or several individuals look the other way—either negligently, or as in our son's case, through a continuous, systematic pattern of ostracization, ridicule, feelings of supremacy and domination on the part of so-called "friends'—ideas that must go the way of the Wicked Witch of the West, melting in water.[1]

In the end, it's not about how many 'likes' or 'followers' a kid has on social media or how popular a given individual may be. It's all about heart, accountability, and the notion that *every life has inherent value*. If, through his story, Donté's truth becomes known, those who suffer in silence will emerge into the light of security, life, and wholeness, and those who turned the other way will, instead, look within and find the answer to the probing question, "why?" Unexpectedly, the answer might point to themselves.

---

[1] Reference to a character in the film *The Wizard of Oz* (1939).

INTRODUCTION

Suffering is deeply personal, and every loss is a tragedy, irrespective of the decedent's stage of life; but when a young person like our happy, well-adjusted, respectful, kind, and deeply loved son ended his own life, the search for reasons loomed large in everyone's incredulous minds. Inferences can be drawn from a trilogy of influences: home, social environment, and school, the latter two working in tandem.

Over the course of three years, we have done intense reflecting in an effort to discover the cause of our son's internal unrest and despair, which surfaced most prominently over the last fifteen months of his life. He had become uncharacteristically sullen and taciturn, though such isolation typically occurs when adolescents go on a soul-searching/ identity expedition during their mid-teens.

For Dont'e, such a transition seemed quite natural, and the subtle changes that we observed did not raise any red flags. He continued to be respectful and gracious to us and his peers (though a little reticent, at times). In hindsight, however, we awakened to the nuances of his metamorphosis from a healthy, content, gregarious little boy into a morose teen who ultimately lost his purpose. Evidence that we later discovered in and around his school and social environment directly gave way to his transformation.

There had to be catalysts for such changes, and since we could not find any indicia of negativity in our family circle (which remained a constant source of support), we had no choice but to look to a system in which clandestine homogeneity—a term that we use to describe a covert preference for sameness in ideology, culture, and perspective—practiced and encouraged by people of nefarious intent to work their way, through systematic threats and manipulation, into our son's psyche and turn him against himself. Unbeknownst to us, peer groups involved in social media were expressly telling our son that he wasn't good enough for this world— or, more precisely, that he was *too* good. In all events, their message was the direct antithesis of our inclusive philosophy.

Events leading up to the tragedy took place over the course of about ten years since we chose Bangor, ME as our home. At the time, we were oblivious to the fact that the community would, somehow, be complicit in breaking our son's spirit. (How could we have known?). Social media is a repository of cliques and societies that lure others into a false narrative of the world—a place that our son did not recognize.

At intervals, Dont'e was berated unjustly for one reason or another, and although he never displayed outward discontent or pain, deliberate marginalization from different sources (i.e., teachers, coaches, and peers) was consuming him from within, until that fateful day when he "could not take it any more."

Throughout Donté's life, we always encouraged him to speak freely about anything on his mind, and prior to his communication with a white supremacist group, he always did. Apparently, however, the bullying that he confronted caused such deep-seated pain and shame that he could not bring himself to confide in anyone. Two calls to a crisis center in Reno, Nevada, just shy of two months before he passed away, resulted in an off-handed dismissal of his suicidal thoughts and plea for help, without any follow-up intervention.

Systemic failure pervaded Donté's world. Bangor High School, the very institution that should have protected our son (and others who have, tragically, followed him in death), turned a blind eye to the bullies who assumed dominion over Donté's innocent life and expressly told him that he "cannot go wrong with suicide." Nothing was done to stop those influences. Our son's death and the horrific, untimely demise of others occurred on the school administration's watch. Instead of taking charge and denouncing supremacist rhetoric, school officials stood by without doing or saying anything.

That omission had reverberant effects. In November 2019, one student's suicide was announced over the high school's PA system, in contravention of experts' recommendations, including that of a clinical psychologist.[2] The school also violated accepted protocols by refusing

---

[2] Pendharkar, Eesha. "Bangor School Leaders Defend Announcement of Student's Suicide by Loudspeaker." *Bangor Daily News*, 12 Dec. 2019, bangordailynews.com/2019/12/12/news/bangor/bangor-school-leaders-defend-announcement-of-students-suicide-by-loudspeaker/.

help from outside mental health professionals (including the Maine chapter of the National Alliance on Mental Illness), stating that the situation was handled appropriately. The administration claimed that "at risk students" had internal support from the school's nurse, guidance counselors, and social workers.[3] Neither parents nor staff could know, conclusively, that such protections were adequate. Many teens are introspective and will not speak to adults about their state of mind—especially when they experience inner turmoil and conflict.

Educators and mental health professionals onsite should be able to detect and prevent the onslaught of hate speech of which we, as parents, can only be made aware when it is too late. Both of us were completely in the dark about social media memes and other forms of cyber communications.

While the First Amendment ensures freedom of speech, rhetoric that evokes panic (i.e., shouting "fire!" in a crowded theater and incitement to violence) are not protected categories. We argue that *endorsing* suicide to a vulnerable mind is incitement to violence—self-annihilation. Where was the school board? Those in authority with the requisite training in the malleability and fragility of young, developing minds must have the foresight to prevent the tragedy of suicide that many in the Bangor community have faced. It takes a multitude to edify and uplift an individual and

---

[3] Id.

same forces to systematically devalue and diminish that person at the height of his formative years.

To make matters worse, basic protocols and procedures went unimplemented, and consequently, we had no recourse to pursue more in-depth investigations in the aftermath of Donté's death. Our frantic requests to state and federal entities went on deaf ears.

This book is intended to be a call to action for those, in the aggregate, who look on and mechanistically apply a blanket set of rules assigned to all, without focusing on the inner workings of vulnerable minds and hearts in crisis.

CHAPTER 1

TRAPPED IN THE VALIDATION TORNADO

A s we write, we are in the throes of a global pandemic. New cases of COVID-19 and tragic death statistics continue to emerge and increase, without any abatement in sight. The circumstances are extremely frightening and unsettling, to say the least. Yet, beneath the surface, away from the media spotlight and the din of pundits' commentaries lurks a parasite more insidious and sinister than we dare to imagine: suicidal ideation and follow-through, causally related to bullying.

The statistics are staggering. Among adolescents aged 15 to 19 years old, suicide is the second leading cause of death in the United States after accidents.[4]

---

[4] Abbott, Brianna. "Youth Suicide Rate Increased 56% in Decade, CDC Says." *The Wall Street Journal* , 17 Oct. 2019, www.citationmachine.net/mla/cite-a-website/manual.

What is happening to our children? Without the ability to vent to expert mental health professionals within our schools or to adults in charge of their well-being, they become isolated and withdrawn. People around them fail to recognize their silent anguish and feelings of purposelessness. Others don't pause in a hallway to inquire how they are doing, so caught up are they in their devices and phones. This age of digital communication, as helpful as it can be, tends to rob everyone of human interaction—real-time face-to-face communication.

As a result, the epidemic of suicide is showing up at alarming rates in our schools. At Utah's Herriman High School, six students took their own lives in less than a year in 2007. These precious lives felt alone, marginalized, 'other' — but no one knew the true depth of their despair. The taboo nature of suicide and the preexisting depression that leads up to that ultimate act of escapism often precludes meaningful exchanges with people with the understanding and wisdom to save lives. Many people erroneously believe that pushing the subject under the rug will, somehow, magically make it disappear. The truth is, however, that engaging in that slight of hand costs lives—indeed, generations— and self-quarantining just does not 'cut it.' We have to rise up and be visible and vocal about the existence of the parasite so as to annihilate it entirely before more of the guardians of our future, our youth—integral, vital parts of the human family—vanish from the earth.

When the death toll rises, we have to heed the call to action. In despair and searching for answers, Herriman students and teachers sprang into action and instituted a Question, Persuade, and Refer ("QPR") program to assist in identifying the signs and symptoms of suicidal tendencies. Students came forward to express their disbelief, hopelessness, and desire to find solutions. Their voices are the hope. In Bangor, voices are silent.

Silence is complacency and complicity. In the words of statesman/philosopher Edmund Burke (1729-1797), "the only thing necessary for the triumph of evil is for good men to do nothing."

The administration and student body at Herriman High are rising to the challenge, knowing that not everyone fits the risk profile (as was the case with Dont'e). As parents, we can only know what we see and perceive through the five senses and our natural filial intuition that guides us in all things. For us, past was prologue. Every behavioral trait that Dont'e had ever exhibited ran directly counter to the profile, and the vague, imperceptible 'signs' that we observed occurred only within the last fifteen months of his life — so minute that we could not distinguish the red flags from the normal everyday incidents of teenaged behavior.

Something has to lie at the heart of what happened to our son, others who followed him in death, and the countless youth who are taking their lives every single day. In the state of Maine, the annual suicide rate is higher than the national average (19.3 v. 14.8 suicides per 100,000). It is the fourth leading cause of death among Maine youth between the ages of 10 to 14, and the second leading cause of death among those aged 15 to 34, and there are four suicides for every one homicide.[5]

Those who are not predisposed to mental health issues or suicidal tendencies must have some kind of trigger. The act is not a random phenomenon—a whim that happens because young people 'just feel like' taking their lives. There is an underlying cause, and that catalyst (along with feelings of vulnerability, self-doubt, and insecurity that naturally attend adolescence) is bullying.

Bullying is defined as the assumption of dominion and control over another by means of verbal or physical aggression or other types of manipulation that cause the victim to feel isolated from his or her peers. This can be due to gossip and rumor-spreading or subliminal suggestive language that causes the individual to feel marginalized. In the worst case scenario, bullying can lead to a sense of hopelessness and lack of belonging to such an extent that the victim loses his or her purpose or place within the peer-group framework, and feels that there is no turning back. After several painstaking internal soul-searching expeditions, we have concluded that this is what occurred in Donté's world.

In today's society, our youth seek 'likes' on social media platforms, where associations with others and how many validations they receive define who they are. Ours is, after all, a capitalistic society, where the greatest commodities are fame, fortune, and financial success. Through the magic of social media, virtual reality is created to the

---

[5] "Suicide In Maine – 2018 Update." *Maine Center for Disease Control and Prevention*, 3 May 2017, https://www.maine.gov/suicide/docs/Lifespan-Data-Brief-2018.pdf.

nth degree— an illusory universe that renders the human mind and soul the most sought-after commodities of all. Vulnerable youth become susceptible to scurrilous attacks on their very being—especially if, heaven forbid, they are different in any way, shape, manner or form.

The lure of being liked and actually receiving approval of a photo, a comment, or a meme create an overwhelming sense of instant gratification, particularly in young minds. The number of 'likes' equates with how much they are valued. When the approval comes pouring in, our children become trapped in the validation tornado—a whirl of gratifying feelings and sensations of self-worth. Conversely, those who are not the recipients of praise are pushed to the periphery, with nowhere to turn. For a brief time, Dont'e dwelled in that realm—a boy who had a solid 3.0 GPA from the beginning of school to the tenth grade, a child who was consistently cheerful, popular, and embraced … until he wasn't.

In his cerebral cortex, the validation tornado went wild. Like others his age, Dont'e yearned for validation, but in the process of seeking acceptance, he fell prey to a group of self-aggrandizing bullies—white supremacists—who had the motive, opportunity, state of mind, and environment in which to thrive. These individuals were his purported friends.

Breeding grounds for bullies are homogeneous communities like Maine, where sameness is the preferred order of the day and any difference, however slight, is shunned. When validation/gratification-seeking synapses begin to fire, and the mirror neurons that create feelings of empathy are diminished. **Empathy**: the feeling that I am you, and you are me. Not only do I feel for you. I also feel with you—*as* you. This is impossible wherever clandestine homogeneity holds sway and is lauded as the norm.

As the supremacists continued to receive 'likes,' they saw a corresponding opportunity to marginalize, become more clandestine in their 'whiteness,' and their capacity to systematically undermine the value of our son (at least, in his vulnerable mind and heart—and, most likely, that of others who had identical susceptibility). Our son did not know how to survive in this superficial world that he knew nothing about.

As we will reveal, adults who were privy to this kind of behavior at Bangor High School did nothing to stop it. They allowed the display of the Nazi salute on school grounds, during school hours, without saying a word. Those who were charged with being role models, therefore, silently facilitated the behavior that led to Donté's ultimate act of self-destruction. As 14th- century English poet, Geoffrey Chaucer questioned in *The Canterbury Tales*, "If gold rusts, what will iron do?"

The adults in charge set an example. They are the stewards of our children's well-being, and when they fail, our youth cannot thrive. Children operate through association, and if negative, destructive behaviors are condoned by the authority figures who are tasked to curb and eliminate them, death and destruction are perpetuated. On Bangor's watch, clandestine homogeneity had a chance to breathe, without systems in place to assist with coping and preventative strategies to bolster the will of our youth to survive and thrive——to unabashedly be their authentic selves.

Questions For Consideration:

- Were school officials afraid of taking a stance against prominent parents and/or students in the community who were/are significant financial sponsors of their educational institution?
- Would they lose face if they said something?
- Was the corrosive dialogue going on in homes, as well, incited by some parents' destructive ideology?
- Would addressing the taboo subject of bullying and the annihilative language of the Weimar Republic resurrected inside a high school cause a disruption in the clichéd environment that everyone wanted to preserve?

Yes to all of the above! Our educators must ensure that identity crises turn into identity acceptance by quashing and preventing the persistent rage of the validation tornado. This entity coerces vulnerable minds into believing that self-worth and personal value are synonymous with sameness and collective 'likes.' Our educators must become emotional climate-change activists who turn the tides and annihilate the tornado before it is too late to save lives!

Dad and Dont'e

CHAPTER 2

THE ERRAND

(Don's Narrative)

June 2006

On a beautiful sunny day, my seraphic, blond-haired four-year-old boy and I had just taken a walk around our neighborhood in Bangor, Maine. At 3:30 p.m., the sun's warmth enveloped us in a welcoming embrace, and all was right with the world. Dont'e, my only child, was the perfect companion. I found supreme fulfillment in being a father and mentor to him, giving him the material, emotional, and psychological sustenance that I never had as a child. He was a gift to my soul, and every day with him was a miracle.

On this particular afternoon, we had a very important, mutual mission: Dont'e would attempt to tie his own shoelaces—a milestone in his precious young life. After a few exertions, my little child succeeded in tying a full bow. Raising his head in my direction, he displayed the most ebullient smile, filled with excitement and pride. Not for one second could I divert my glance from the radiance of that innocent expression. Mesmerized and floored by what outsiders might have perceived to be a routine moment, I instantly felt *whole*. Every ounce of denigration that I had once experienced as a child dissipated as I climbed to the zenith of the world—*with that one smile.*

Suddenly, there was a clap of thunder, followed by nature's most beautiful light show in summer during a rainstorm. Lightning cascaded across the sky, piercing through the clouds with insistent will and determination. The scene was awe-inspiring.

"Dont'e! Come out here to the porch and sit with me. You *have* to see this!"

My son paused his playful activities and rushed to my side. "What is it, Dad?"

"Look at this incredible thunder-and-lightning performance that nature is putting on for us!" I exclaimed, placing my arm around Donté's shoulder.

There, in silence, the two of us sat together for about twenty minutes—the most sacred interlude of awe that I can recall in my lifetime.

April 2007-2009

Seasons passed, and my son always heeded the call of springtime, intoned in a particular species of bird calls. To this day, I cannot name those lyrical creatures, but Dont'e and I always recognized their song, "Spring Is Coming!" That sound always gave us pause to stop, listen, and reflect on the undeniable power of nature's gifts. More than once, I caught my son ceasing in his tracks and just listening, knowing, understanding, taking the world into his heart.

End of August 2017

Pitch darkness. Without warning, the world was devoid of light shows and songbirds, just as the spark within my soul had been precipitously extinguished. Dont'e was gone. As usual, the end of summer came quickly, with temperatures dropping down to about 50 degrees at night. It was 8:30 p.m., and I had been running an errand. My mind reeled with grief at Kelly's and my tragic loss, and I desperately needed to decompress. So, on the way home, instead of driving on a smooth road with two or three intersection traffic lights, I decided to take the slow route through Essex Street, a long, dimly lit, daunting path with endless stop signs.

About half a mile along, I noticed an object in the middle of the street, which I initially perceived to be some kind of animal; but as I approached, I clearly saw a human being with small body contours similar to those of a teenager. Closer scrutiny revealed, however, that this was not a teen at all, but a toddler.

Hurriedly, I pulled over to the side of the road, exited my car, and approached the boy, a towhead (just like Dont'e!), wearing shorts and a t-shirt, without shoes. *Am I in my right mind, or am I hallucinating?* I thought to myself. *Why is this child out here, at this hour, in the middle of the road, alone in the dark?* Bewildered, I surveilled the silent, barren street. There was not a soul in sight, and one could hear a pin drop. Once again, I quietly ruminated. *In my sorrow, in my circumstances, in my midst, this little boy appears out of nowhere—a child who strongly resembles my son. Is this a sign? Did Dont'e send him to me?*

Quickly gathering my thoughts, I realized that the child was not in distress—just fascinated by his surroundings. My hope of communicating with him was dashed when I realized that he was an infant, incapable of speech or reasoning. Carefully moving him out of the road, I glanced toward the house in front of where I had discovered him, assuming it was his dwelling. Like the surroundings, the home was enshrouded in stillness.

I had better call 911, I said to myself, reaching for my phone. Just then, I heard the sound of someone running down the street, and a gentleman stopped right in front of me.

"Who are you?" I asked, maintaining a cautious distance.

"I am his father," the man replied, nodding in the little boy's direction.

After several minutes of questioning the stranger, I sincerely believed that he was, in fact, the boy's father. Incredibly, the child lived a full two blocks from the location in which I had found him. He had let himself out of the house and wandered into the middle of the road, at the mercy of the elements and all kinds of malevolent forces. I dread to think about the frightening scenarios that could have ensued *had I not arrived at that pivotal moment.* What if I had decided to take the shortcut home? What if I had decided not to go on my errand at all? What if? The possibilities were endless.

Emotions even more innumerable churned within me. I had no doubt that the phenomenal, inexplicable event had more meaning than mere mortals could comprehend. Just at that time of indescribable devastation and loss, an unknown blond-haired angel wandered into the road— spurred, perhaps, by pure fascination and a sense of adventure—or on some errand of his own, mandated by the Divine Kingdom.

I remember
my first day
without you...

I've never
been the
same.

www.memorates.com

CHAPTER 3

LITTLE ANGEL BABY

(Kelly's Narrative)

When Dont'e was born, he had a tiny cross etched in his forehead. Not many people noticed it, but Don's niece, who was about five years old at the time, always remarked. "Look, Aunt Kelly! Dont'e has a little cross right there!" Her tiny finger would gently point to the cross-shaped marking on my son's head. "He's a little angel baby!" she would exclaim.

Raised Catholic, I always believed in the possibility that my son was actually anointed with sweetness, and throughout his short life, he exhibited angelic traits. When I changed his diaper as an infant, he would look up at the ceiling with an intense stare and giggle, animatedly moving his little hands. *He must be seeing something up there!* I thought to myself.

Just before our son entered the world, my brother Shawn had departed—far too soon. Naturally, I was grieving, and when I looked at Dont'e and he would laugh and be silly like his uncle, I would think that, perhaps, their spirits crossed. They were so much alike.

Always a jokester, Dont'e would tease me about my neat-freak habits—in the most loving way. On occasion, while I was making my bed to perfection, tucking in the sheets and pillows in pristine fashion, I would see my son nonchalantly amble past the room and look in. All of a sudden, he would backtrack, charge on the bed, and ruffle the sheets into a sorry mess.

"Dont'e!" I would call out, silently laughing to myself at his playfulness.

My son never meant harm, and he loved all living beings, however small. Ants who were so fortunate to find their way into our house were given an unlikely second chance in Donté's hand, as he slowly and carefully transported them out the door—if only to live a few more seconds.

Mosquitoes that he brushed away knew that he was an ally, even when he was annoyed that he could not stay and sleep outside one summer evening on his new trampoline, with me at his side.

"I told you that the mosquitoes would eat us alive!" I said, laughing.

"They are just too much!" he replied, reaching up to tousle my hair.

Now, I'm aware that maybe, when I feel something touching my hair, it's not the wind at all . . .

Mom and Dont'e

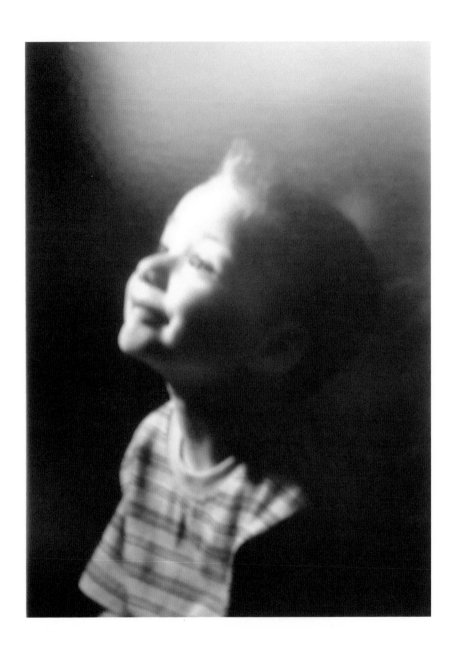

CHAPTER 4

WIDE OPEN SPACES

June 27, 2001 (Rhode Island)

D ont'e entered the world smiling at the sun, a light that radiated from within. All that ensued from that first smile was the product of love and guidance. With each successive generation, those who come before seek to provide a better life for the torchbearers— those who carry a new world on their shoulders, hopefully one of renewed hope and enlightenment—a planet where inclusiveness is the norm, where one and 'the other' become a unified whole.

Dont'e embodied the essence of humanity's finest attributes: inclusive, social interaction, acceptance of everyone he encountered, a humble (but grounded) sense of self, the ability to draw people in, engage, laugh, and conceptual-

ize— all while often becoming the center of attention—
without a hint of braggadocio. He had a fierce wit, coupled
with an impish twinkle in his eyes that made everyone feel
at ease around him. What he gleaned from life, he shared
without restraint or guardedness and always spoke openly
to us, his parents, about subjects of interest or *anything* that
happened to be on his mind. He was always a good boy,
never given to bursts of frustration or anger. Universally
loved by everyone who knew him, he maintained a sweet,
self-deprecating demeanor, always ready to reach out.

August 2005

Our family needed a change of scenery. Dont'e was
four, and we wanted him to have a better life than either of
us had experienced—a sense of community in a less popu-
lated state, with fresh air, less traffic, and more wide open
spaces.

After copious research, Don found Bangor, Maine, where
the housing market seemed more enticing when compared
with Rhode Island's much higher mortgage rates. Eager to
benefit from a home investment and enhance our quality
of life, we embarked on a new chapter. Our goals were
modest and realistic. We knew that no place would be uto-
pia, but we hoped that our son would be able to spread his
wings there . . . just like the little bluebird that flew into
our car window the day before we left. Dont'e laughed and
smiled at the spritely creature in his midst, raising his tiny
hands and following it with his eyes, as though it were the

greatest treasure on earth. That was our positive sign (or so we thought).

Soaring on the wings of good intention, we arrived in Maine in the late summer, barely anticipating how icy and cold the winters would be. Naturally, we had experienced winter before, but nothing could have prepared us for the Bangor snowfalls and bitter temperatures. Notwithstanding the learning curve and adjustment period, we made the most of family activities, such as skiing, sledding, and watching local football games.

Eventually, as Dont'e matured, he became involved in football (from the second to tenth grades), demonstrating strength and skill equal to—and often surpassing—his peers, despite his physical limitations due to slight cerebral palsy (which did not, in any way, hamper his ability to do anything at all).

In summer, we took every advantage of the good weather, and explored many areas in and around the Maine, including Acadia Park, Bar Harbor, and Camden. Dont'e loved visiting Old Orchard Beach, where we rented a hotel room and enjoyed Fourth of July celebrations at the beach, including an amazing fireworks display.

Yet, for all our attempts at fun and assimilation in our new environment, we sensed a pervasive pattern of alienation—the constant attempt to *other-ize* people who were non-natives to Bangor.

"You're not a true Maine-iac," some would say. "You have an accent, Kelly." Oh, you're from Rhode Island, Don? No wonder you sound harsh!"

Though subtle at first and requiring keenness to detect, these comments became increasingly troubling as time went by. One afternoon, Principal Babcock of the Fruit Street School stood at the top of a hill near the pick-up area where parents awaited their children at the end of the school day. Slowly, Dont'e put on his snow pants and boots and ambled up the hill, hampered by his weaker right foot. "Come on, speedy!" the principal called out snidely.

Kelly stood there in amazement and pain for Dont'e, then only five. Neither dignified the comment with a reply, and our son was characteristically stoic, shrugging off the principal's disrespect. In hindsight, we believe that as a school official who should have been committed to his students' emotional and physical well-being, the principal fell short. Had we been in a position to fire him for that off-handed statement, we would not have hesitated to do so. He had no idea how emotionally scarring his conduct was toward an innocent boy in his formative years.

And the disparagement did not stop there. The following year, Donté's second-grade teacher, Mrs. Pinnett, called us out on his "accent." He was only six and didn't have any accent. Apparently, the community shockingly had a need to feel superior, even in the presence of the most impressionable minds.

On yet another occasion, Mrs. Pinkham, a teacher at the Mary Snow School, barraged my son with a fit of screams, rendering him inconsolable. We immediately arranged a meeting with the teacher and the school principal, during which the teacher offered up an apology. Her conduct shook Dont'e to the core. Never had we seen him in that state, his little frame quaking as he got into our car to go home. After that incident, we became more aware of the fact that Dont'e did not fit into a community that tended to unjustifiably berate and belittle him. We were not like 'them,' so we were relegated to the margins.

Despite our feelings of unrest, we never ceased to be engaged in Donté's life and cultivate his sense of security and belonging. Don always asked him about school and what was happening around him. One day, when he was in the fourth grade, Don asked our son about his first days of school.

"The teacher misspelled my name," Dont'e replied.

"Really? Did you say anything?" Don inquired.

"No."

"Well, when you get a chance, just ask her to change the spelling.

Dont'e nodded.

At a parent-teacher conference, Don approached the teacher. "You know," he began, "Dont'e mentioned that you spelled his name incorrectly. He was concerned about that, and I suggested he mention it to you. Did he?"

"Yes, he did," the teacher said.

"And did you change the spelling?"

"No, I forgot," she answered dismissively.

We are baffled as to how a fourth-grade teach could "forget" such a matter. The incident was just another indication of the deliberate passive indifference that we encountered.

Concerned, Bereaved Parents' Analysis:

Ridicule, uncontrolled, inexplicable, unjustifiable rage, and dismissiveness have no place in the halls of pedagogy. Those charged with the solemn responsibility of serving society as educators must be trained in dealing with various situations and conditions pertaining to each individual child in the school system. Differences must be celebrated, not mocked or maligned. A child's innocent mind and heart are vulnerable, and the ways in which adult authority figures treat them have an everlasting impact on their developmental health and well-being. A child in tears, without cause, is a marginalized child—unjustly called out at the whim of an educator who should make that child's welfare paramount. During school hours, parents want to know that their children are safe and that their physical and mental health are in the hands of people who care. Words and actions matter, especially from those whose job it is to set an example for growing minds.

Fortunately, there were some who recognized Donté's qualities. His first-grade teacher, Mrs. Reynolds, aptly described him as "a kind, cheerful child who is eager to learn and do well." However, as astute as that teacher was, words of approbation for our son and family were few and far in between.

Other incidents pointed to general aloofness in the community among our peers and others with whom we conversed, who evinced disdain at our way of life, how we dressed our son and styled his hair, our home décor, and other superficial matters, which we essentially 'took with a grain of salt.' Dont'e consistently ignored the unpleasant-ries altogether—at least, on the surface.

Our son's independent spirit seemed to obliterate his need for peer approval, and as social as he was, he seemed perfectly content with being alone at times. He was a mas-ter at building with Legos®, creating impressive structures in his room, for hours. He particularly liked everything *Star Wars* and built intricate, magnificent structures that his 'friends' proceeded to smash when they visited—the beginning of the bullying.

"You really have to do something about that, Dont'e! Why don't you say anything to them? It's not fair!" Kelly admonished him.

"It's OK, Mom. I'm good," our son would reply, shrugging.

It's not that he didn't understand. On the contrary, he knew all too well what was going on: jealousy. He just wanted to let everything run off of his shoulders like water on a duck's back and didn't want to draw attention to him-self. In his eyes, humanity was inherently *good*. He reached out to everyone, those who were "popular" and especially the "underdog," marginalized and alone. He had a par-ticular affinity for African-Americans who, in the predomi-nantly Caucasian community of Bangor, stood on society's periphery. In fact, one of Donté's best friends whom he met at the local YMCA was African-American. Our son and his friend developed a true soul-connection.

Donté's exceptionalism earned him a humanitarian award when he befriended a marginalized student who was often alone and not a member of any particular group or 'clique.' For Dont'e, being kind was not unusual, but rather, a way of life. He didn't strive to be as he was. He simply was himself, without any predetermination or expectation of reciprocal tolerance or understanding. He truly believed that his way of thinking and feeling were natural—and for him it *was*—genuine, uncontrived.

Slowly, however, he discovered that the ideological gaps between his perspectives and others' were as wide and vast as a cavernous abyss.

CHAPTER 5

THE TIGER'S TOOTH

Donté's stance on inclusiveness derived from the ideals that we instilled in him since his infancy. Kelly always pointed out that "everyone laughs, cries, smiles and suffers in the same way, everyone puts on their pants in the same way, and no one is better or set above anyone else." He took that lesson to heart.

For hours, Don would sit in his office with his son at his side, listening attentively as he spoke of life, in general, and cautioned him about the ways of the world. Don knew that Donté was different in demeanor and outlook than others his age, and he warned him about the ways in which people could suddenly change all of a sudden. Donté took it all in, but in his heart, he couldn't help but adhere to his idyllic worldview.

Friends loved him and gathered around to listen as he imparted knowledge or offered an idea. He never shied away from anyone, and always wore a smile on his face, ready to lend a helping hand or brighten someone's day.

In reminiscing about Dont'e, one of his closest elementary and secondary-school friends, Lindsey, expressed the following sentiments:

"What I remember the most about Dont'e is his kind heart. When we were in elementary school, Dont'e and I would play tag and other playground games at recess. Dont'e was nice to everyone he met and he never excluded anyone.

I also remember doing art projects with him in class. He was full of light and fun. He was kind to everyone and inspired those around him to be happier and enjoy the moment."

Aside from his fun-loving spirit, our son exhibited remarkable empathy for his peers and everyone he met, reaching out in their times of need to offer support and solace. In his young life, he understood that none of us is an island unto ourselves but part of a collective experience.

In a school and national poetry competition, Dont'e chose to recite a poem entitled "America," by Claude McKay, written in 1921. Ironically, the first seven lines of the poem echoed Donté's worldview and chillingly presaged the events that ultimately led to our tragedy:

Although she feeds me bread of bitterness,
And sinks into my throat her tiger's tooth,
Stealing my breath of life, I will confess
I love this cultured hell that tests my youth.
Her vigor flows like tides into my blood,
Giving me strength erect against her hate,
Her bigness sweeps my being like a flood.

Our son's analysis bespoke his intense patriotism. "Claude loved America no matter how it is," Dont'e wrote. "The meaning of the poem is showing respect for America, [and] the title is the name of the greatest country."

Now that our son is gone, however, a more in-depth reading eerily points to a metaphor for his circumstances—a harbinger of the bitterness that he would encounter—despite his love of people and efforts to extract life's nectar. The treachery that sank its teeth into him robbed him of his idealistic visions of humanity— and of life itself. Yet, he stood silent and firm, enveloped by the world's greatness and beauty—until that fateful day when he "couldn't take it anymore."

We assume—and can only hope— that when Dont'e read McKay's poem, he was not feeling the sting of discrimination himself. He loved all people, but perhaps, when he read the verse, he had already faced disillusionment in his peer circle that tested his fortitude. We will never know exactly when the despair began—that terrible moment that took him to a place of no return.

Yes, there were sweet memories: swimming with dolphins in the Caribbean, the pride he felt in briefly studying the martial arts, the joy of playing with his interlocking toy bricks and constructing magnificent structures, running with friends in the yard, a *Star Wars*-themed birthday, going on errands with Dad, opening Christmas gifts with Mom—all the miracles of life that any young child could possibly want. Yet, inexplicably, he became embroiled in an alternate universe so insufferable that he felt compelled to find and orchestrate an exit. Tragically, not a soul who heard or sensed his pleas for help was there to save him.

January 12, 2017 (Bangor, ME.)

Dont'e texted a suicide crisis call center in Reno, Nevada, remaining in conversation for one hour, from 3:10 p.m. to 4:10 p.m. A youth who *never* exhibited signs of depression or mental illness in his life, Dont'e provided the following information:

"Hi, I'm Dont'e Izzo. I'm thinking of killing myself. My depression and stuff [are] building up really hard. I feel that I've just been taking up space for the last half year. I'm thinking of a plan of killing myself, including hanging, if I obtain no gun soon. The only reason I haven't done it yet is because I don't want my parents to be sad."

Subsequently, our son spoke to another call center representative, and in answer to the question, "How are you now?", he replied, "I'm okay right now."

None of the risk factors or adverse health problems that typically lead to such tragedies even remotely surfaced in Donté's case. Only after he passed did we tragically discover that he had fallen victim to the 'tiger's tooth,' that "sank into [his] throat, stealing [his] breath of life," leaving us stunned and in unspeakable grief.

One might justifiably wonder what the affirmative assertion, "I'm okay now" actually meant and whether it called for professional intervention and follow-up. While the statement signified that suicide was not a clear and present danger *at that moment*, there was *an imminent risk* that at some point in the future, the person reaching out for help had the intention and desire of following through.

Some irrational thought or diminished capacity caused the individual to formulate ideas of self-annihilation. In these instances, there is a continuous risk at play, necessitating incisive and swift follow-ups, which should occur within the first twenty-four to forty-eight hours of the call or text. Even a declaration of suicidal intentions, without more, merits further investigation.

However, in Donté's case, protocol was not followed in any guise, either by phone calls, texts, or visits to our home. Such a dereliction of duty resulted in our son's death by self-induced asphyxiation on March 6, 2017. All the while, we remained completely in the dark.

A subsequent inquiry into what occurred on the day of Donté's text reveals that the call center's representative was "overwhelmed" with work, but promised to "do better next time." Yet further probing uncovered the fact that in the previous year, almost to the day, on November 3, 2016, follow-ups on an astonishing forty-three suicide-related calls were not performed, and no one assumed accountability!

If we are not careful, our children will continue to be statistics, victims of senseless, avoidable tragedies when those charged with their care and safety engage in gross negligence by failing to carry out their responsibilities. There cannot be a "next time" because the opportunity may not arise. As in our son's case, it may be too late to act. The present moment is of the essence—***even if no present danger exists***. Call center representatives cannot know what goes on in an individual's mind without actually following up or being on the scene. Thought leads to intention, and in most cases, intention translates into action.

In most instances, there are signs of the intention-action combination that leads to suicide. Donté's demeanor and the subtle changes in his behavior were so imperceptible (especially to his intensely involved parents) as to be considered inconsequential. However, he took the initiative to call the crisis call center in Reno Nevada, purportedly a foremost authority source, seeking help; but instead of coming to his rescue, the powerful tiger swallowed him whole.

Dont'e
Izzo

Age 15

CHAPTER 6

A CULTURE OF ISOLATION AND ALIENATION

The Isolationist Character of Indifference

Asociety that turns a blind eye to the subjugation, diminished self-worth, and ultimate isolation of others is complicit in a heinous crime: the death of innocence. Had the Reno crisis call center representatives taken one minute or less to place a call, send an email, or text, our son could have been alive today. That call was Donté's cry for help. Speculatively, we can hear our son making that plea, in his heart (with more words than he could express), "Please tell my parents because I can't. I don't have the words. They might not understand. They're of a different generation, and if I say anything, they'll raise hell. I'll be embarrassed in front of my friends and my school. They may even be angry that I associated with those white supremacist guys. I'm not like them, but they lured me in. They make me say, do, and think about things that my parents would never allow. That Confederate flag! Oh, boy! Mom would be pissed!" (He actually said those words about the flag.)

We knew our son, and we guided him through a different world—a place where everyone has a right to live and express themselves authentically, according to their individual truths and practices—as long as no one else is injured in the process.

If a community—or a world— hopes to survive, a path must be created for all individuals to coexist and learn from each other, without pigeonholing certain groups for their immutable characteristics—the very attributes that make all of us beautifully diverse.

Recently, we learned that the Department of Justice ("the Department") cited Maine's Department of Health and Human Services for its violation of Title II of the Americans with Disabilities Act of 1990 ("ADA") 42 U.S.C. §§ 12131–12134. The Department stated that the Complainant's special needs son was at serious risk of segregation from the community, due to the limiting of disability services. Such isolation would force the individual into a group home, denying him his rightful place in an integrated society. [6]

---

[6] "Justice Department Finds Maine In Violation of Law For Limiting Disability Services." *Bangor Daily News*, 20 Feb. 2020, bangordailynews. com/2020/02/19/mainefocus/justice-department-finds-maine-in-violation-of-law-for-limiting-disability-services/.

Analogously (though in a different context), Dont'e was relegated to the fringes of society by his peer group whom he believed to be his friends. The very individuals who led him to communicate with supremacists (including his best friend, GH, who associated with them) were the same people who once ran in our yard, enjoyed paintballing, going to the park, and many other activities, which we lovingly orchestrated. In just a few short years, that idyllic universe collapsed and deconstructed into a supremacist narrative that was diametrically opposed to Donté's way of life.

May 2017 ~ How Words Destroy

Through data recovery performed on Donté's cell phone after his passing, Don unearthed the catalysts and causes of his state of mind: the most hateful memes and words that rattled him to the core, belittling and undermining the sanctity of his life. The details of how Dont'e became involved in a dialogue with such a group is unclear, to this day. However, we can deduce that he came into communication with someone with the social media name "radiant memes" (i.e., Peter Blackwell.) through Gabe Higgins, his best friend since childhood, who traveled in the same social circles as Peter. The three were seen together, particularly during the latter part of Donté's life.

Whoever believes that words don't matter must see these despicable depictions and read the verbiage to understand what happened to the gentlest, kindest heart in the world. Dont'e didn't want to be like his detractors; so, in the depths of his despair, he believed that his only recourse was to distance himself from the perpetrators whose ideology he abhorred. What he did not realize, in his impressionable psyche, was that, as Brazilian novelist Paolo Coelho contends, "haters are confused admirers who want to be like you." They, too, are trapped in the validation tornado, and they fallaciously believe that dominating others will make them more powerful.

The following visuals and statements can shatter any civilized human being's heart, but they must be shown to shed light on the evil-doers.

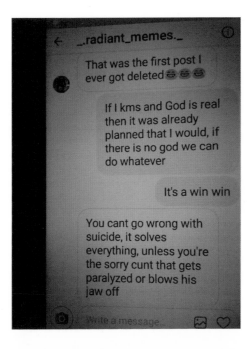

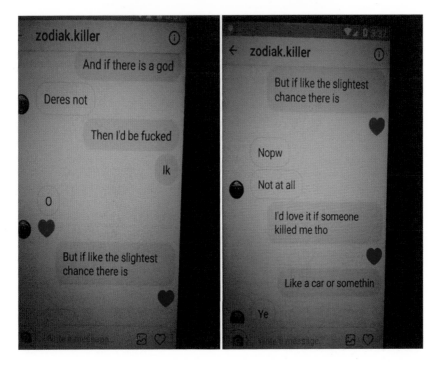

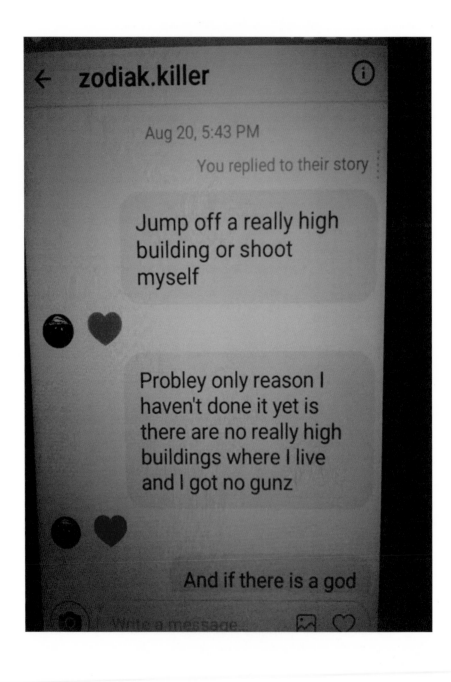

Analysis:

Imagine that the depictions above could be—and were—allowed to exist in the 21st century! Imagine that in 2017, the Nazi salute reared its ugly head, yet again—this time on school grounds (a venue where young minds are supposed to be shielded from nefarious behavior), while people walked by without doing or saying anything. The young student standing next to Peter Blackwell was wearing a Ku Klux Klan hood—in plain daylight, on school premises. How can those around them hold their heads to the light when they are complicit in the gesture?

The perpetrators of evil wanted to believe that after seven and a half decades following World War II, they could resurrect the darkness. Particularly Peter, with the label "radiant memes," was responsible for this despicable ideology, born of an inferiority complex and the desire to subjugate others for the purpose of his own self-aggrandizement. Small minds, however, never win. There are forces far greater than they that obliterate their position.

Notably, Dont'e deleted a text before concluding that suicide was the only option, irrespective of the existence of God. He did so because he was functioning in a vacuum, a bottomless pit where those in authority did nothing to save him. Significantly, Donté's references to suicide evoke heart emojis from his detractors.

Further, the convictions of a group of people are enshrined in their legislation—the codification of their mode of conduct, how they treat each other, and the penalties for transgression. Consider Maine's hate crimes law:

17 MRS §2931 provides, "A person may not, by force or threat of force, *intentionally* injure, intimidate or interfere with, or intentionally attempt to injure, intimidate or interfere with or intentionally oppress or threaten any other person in the free exercise or enjoyment of any right or privilege, secured to that person by the Constitution of Maine or laws of the State or by the United States Constitution or laws of the United States." Violation of this statute is a Class D crime, punishable by up to *364 days incarceration and a $2,000 fine* [emphasis added].

"A Class D crime" is only a misdemeanor, punishable by one day less than a year and a $2,000 fine. The state, therefore, does not consider intentional oppression, threats, and manipulation to be a felonious intent crime. Our young people and others are dying, and the legislature imposes a slap on the wrist. Some states, such as New York and California, impose much harsher penalties for such acts.

In Donté's detractors' case, they committed such acts in plain sight, without so much as a verbal reproach. If laws are paper straws, the public suffers. We are suffering!

Dont'e Became Embroiled In the Hateful Rhetoric

Every diatribe and hateful word was the product of cowards' foolery, but our son was too innocent and vulnerable to appreciate that he was above the fray—that his value was not measured by the approval of peers or the number of 'likes' that he received. While the professionals turned away, our son was entrapped in hate, desperately trying to find a way out. He was the victim of instigation and odious rhetoric that made him feel like an outsider.

Instead of talking, he kept the pain to himself, while holding fast to the notions of inclusion that we taught him—until he witnessed the narrative break down—and so did he.

"What if God is real?" he wrote. "If I kill myself and God is real then it was already planned that I would."

The context in which the white supremacists wrote specifically endorsed suicide for him, and those who perpetuated that crime infused their sinister instructions with the claim that God does not exist. It should come as no surprise to anyone observing such behavior that, quite apart from and unrelated to the First Amendment right to worship or not to practice a religious faith as one pleases, the thugs who espoused atheism could not imagine a divine entity above themselves. How we wish that Dont'e could have realized that such inflated egoism is, in reality, an inverse inferiority complex, and people who loathe others for their so-called "differences" in truth despise themselves.

Donté's Vulnerability

By associating with the bullies, Dont'e was being manipulated and untrue to himself, and that realization most likely made him feel sad and hopeless, seeking a place in the world, without refuge.

Yet another post, written by one of the supremacists in 2014, read, "Soon I will begin alien isolation." It is worth noting here that Donté's avatar was a green alien, modeled after a figure that he carried around with him. Nearly one year to the day when he ended his life, Dont'e was in a chatroom where no one was addressing him. He acknowledged this by saying, "Not once did anyone mention me in this conversation. Got to go."

The following group chat took place in January 15, 2016 between our son and five other boys: Nason Vassiliev, Declan Riordan, William Tobin, Ben Candelosi, and Cecil Wilson-Charuk. Dont'e knew these individuals since Kindergarten. He had no reason to believe that they would shun him, but they so blatantly and cruelly ignored his presence that he felt he was in another world.

The content of the chat is deeply reviling and perverse, beginning with its title. The communications were so far afield from the ideologies with which our son was raised. Therefore, we choose to display only excerpts—the points of origin of our son's tragic end.

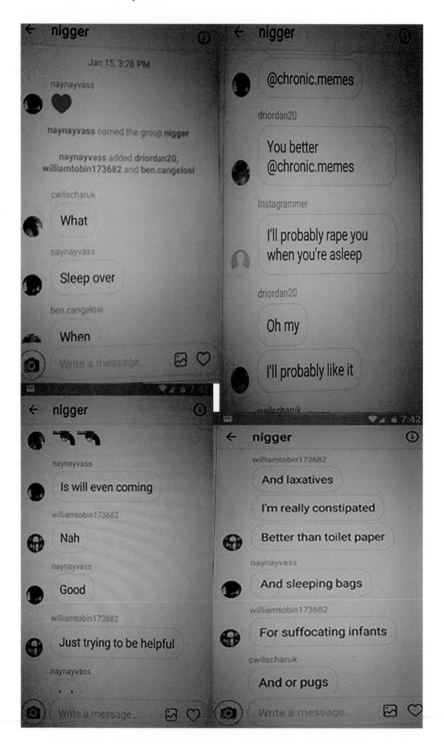

Recently, we revisted the above posts, and memories began to flow—along with epiphanies. More than ever, we realized that Nason was the organizer of this group, and we feel that he was a predominent figure in the latter days of our son's life. He knew about and was among those who encouraged Donté's state of mind that led to his final act of self-annihilation. "How to know when to kill yourself," the instigator entitled one post, while completely failing to address Dont'e. This type of sinister, subliminal tactic pointed to complicity in luring our son into an abyss of isolation.

Upon reflection, we deduced that Nason's above conversations mirrored that of the "zodiak.killer" identity, referenced on page 58. Previously, we had no idea who the latter individual might be, but the tone and tenor of Nason's words, coupled with his failure to address Dont'e in the above-referenced chat—points to that probability.

Unlike Dont'e, Nason and the others were preconditioned to hate. The boys went to elementary school together, and in the third grade, Nason wanted to form an "I Hate [Name Omitted] Club," designed to target a bully in the school. Our son was not capable of formulating such ideas or intentions. How can *any* eighth-grader entertain such notions? Clandestine homogenity was—and remains—ingrained in the fabric of that society. "Clubs," "cliques . . ." Those are the buzz words.

At the end of the chat, the mastermind and his cohorts (including Peter Blackwell) had completed their mission. "Alien isolation" had taken place. Shunned and alone,

Dont'e said, "GG" ("Got to go.") Tragically, not one responsible adult in our son's immediate environment came to his rescue, and four other students later died as a result of such hateful conduct.

Imagine the pain of an adolescent ostracized by peers who, in his mind, had been his 'friends' since childhood! Try to conjure the devastation that their deliberate rejection had on his young, impressionable mind. Such cruelty, when left unchecked, is as lethal as any weapon.

Our son's worldview was shattered, and the evil deed was complete. From that moment on, Dont'e was never the same.

The subtle clues of his despair escaped us, as he had not fundamentally changed. He was the same adorable, respectful, loving child we had always known. Yet, he endured, in silence, painfully harboring an ominous secret: the systematic devaluation of his precious life through the subliminal mantras of hate and destruction, signaling wanton, depraved indifference to human life.

"Alien isolation" had taken place. Tragically, not one responsible adult in our son's immediate environment came to his rescue, and in the aftermath, four other youths took their own lives.

The Truth

In his 1989 book, *Seat of the Soul*, acclaimed author Gary Zukav points out the power of intention and its purpose in evoking and promoting authenticity of the self. He emphasizes that every thought and feeling is motivated by intention—a cause that is inextricably bound with an effect. Every word and deed is charged with the energy of intention, which breaks down into one of two emotions: love or fear.

Undoubtedly, fear was the motivating factor behind the criminal conspiracy of the supremacists to isolate our son and induce his self-annihilation. *A criminal conspiracy is an agreement between two or more parties to carry out a felonious intention. There's that word again—intention_—and what more overwhelming evidence of their intention could have surfaced than Peter Blackwell's statement, "suicide is your best option?"*

Of startling note is Donté's statement, "I'd love it if someone killed me though," indicating that he did not have the heart, temperament, or mental state to take his own life, and that he had an ingrained sense of God, which ran directly counter to his suicidal ideation. However, events had escalated so quickly, and the dialogue was so insistent and insidious, that he felt desperate, trapped in the rhetoric of those who persistently devalued his life.

Abnegation of Responsibility

To make matters worse, adults surrounding Dont'e did nothing to stop the hateful rhetoric, of which they must have been aware. Like his peers, our son remained at school for more hours than he did at home. He was on the watch of educators who were tasked to observe and keep bullying in check and hold the instigators to account. We found the incendiary posts *after* the tragedy, and events transpired very quickly, without the slightest hint of evidence that our boy was in a downward spiral.

Call to Action

Adults, teachers, school administrators, principals: Listen, learn, rise up and protest! Don't turn a blind eye and allow the children in our communities to die. Vindicate the victims of hate in a blaze of counterpoints. This is the twenty-first century, and enmity has no place in our brave new world, in which we shall all awaken to the fact that the human spirit is greater than and above all hatred. Please heed the following words—our answer to the ignorance that took our son's life:

"DARKNESS CANNOT DRIVE OUT DARKNESS; ONLY LIGHT CAN DO THAT. HATE CANNOT DRIVE OUR HATE; ONLY LOVE CAN DO THAT" ~ Dr. Martin Luther King, Jr.

"YES, GOD IS REAL! "GOD GIVES ME HOPE THAT THERE IS SOMETHING GREATER THAN US, SOMETHING BETTER AND BIGGER THAN THE HERE AND NOW, THAT CAN HELP US LIVE." ~ Mattie Stepanek.

"LEARN FROM YESTERDAY, LIVE FOR TODAY, HOPE FOR TOMORROW. THE IMPORTANT THING IS NOT TO STOP QUESTIONING." ~ Albert Einstein.

Question! Don't sugarcoat. Stand up and react! Don't turn away because it is politically or socially expedient. Do what is right, not what is convenient. These are our posts and mantras—now and for all time!

CHAPTER 7

LIGHT AND SHADOW

The Great Escape, 2014

As stated above, "alien isolation" began just after Dont'e and Don had returned to Bangor from Florida for the seventh and eighth-grade school years (2014-2015). Sadly, two years earlier, yet another blatantly offensive comment (this time expressed by Dont-é's English teacher, Pamela Baldus, of the William S. Cohen School) inspired their escape. Without authority or a background in psychology, the teacher described Dont'e as "having a predisposition for juvenile delinquency." That assertion was a deliberate attack, without any factual basis. The teacher offered nothing to corroborate her uncalled-for charge. Slowly, incrementally, she had added another drop of poison to the brew.

In all events, we knew better, and Don would not stand for any of it. Finding an opportunity to extricate Dont'e from what we perceived to be a toxic environment, he decided to take him to see an investment property that he had purchased in Cape Coral. So, with Stewie, a Chinese water dragon (Donté's hypoallergenic substitute for a much-wanted dog or cat) perched comfortably on his head, he and Dad drove off to the Sunshine State.

Both Dont'e and Stewie thrived in their new environment. We put our house in Maine up for sale, thinking that Florida would become our new home. Kelly worked for the Red Cross at the time, and had the freedom to travel and visit the boys whenever she pleased. "Let's see what happens," we told our son. "If you make the honor roll two years in a row and you want to go back to Maine, we'll return."

Anything for our son. We never questioned or denied him an opportunity. His heart's desires were ours. In those two memorable years, Dont'e *did* make the honor roll, played football, and ran cross country. At least twice a week, he and Dad would go running at Ft. Myers Beach and over the Ft. Myers Bridge—priceless bonding and quality time—confidential chats, good food, and beautiful scenery—to and from their destinations. Don was so grateful to have that time and had reservations about leaving, but Maine seemed to beckon. Dont'e wanted to return. He missed his friends. So we conceded, never imagining what awaited us there.

A Freedom Offering, June 2016

Once the property had been renovated and sold at a good profit, the two returned to Bangor. Because Dont'e exceeded his father's expectations academically and socially, bound by the strongest moral ethic, Don purchased three snowmobiles and a trailer, specifically for him. Our boy was so well-behaved, respectful, and grounded that giving him a bit of independence seemed like a natural step in his evolution.

So in 2016, Don set his sights on Utah for a job prospect. "I won't be here to oversee you as I have for the last fourteen years of your life, but I'll call home every night—or every second evening—to check in. I love you!" Don said. Like Kelly, Don trusted Dont'e implicitly. In more ways than one, he had earned that confidence.

Dont'e approved and on July 28, 2016, Don departed for Utah, with a report date of August 8th. With the football season approaching and Donté's attendance at a football camp in late summer, all seemed to be proceeding according to plan. Dont'e clearly exhibited a team-player spirit, both as an athlete and as a Junior Reserve Officers' Training Corps ("JROTC") member. Ostensibly, the rigors of training would be difficult for one with Donté's physical challenges (specifically, slight weakness and palsy in his right foot). However, he rose to every occasion with remarkable alacrity and even surpassed some of his fellow JROTC members in strength and ability.

His keen sense of citizenship was fueled by his JROTC activities and by his innate, natural love of country, which his high school principal described as "not usually shown by high school students." He also became involved in the Bangor Veterans Day Parade, with the hope of someday joining the military, following in Don's footsteps.

Degradation and Distinction, November 2016

At the start of football season, after returning to Bangor, Coach Al Mosca approached Dont'e as he sat on the sidelines with an injury. "How long are you gonna be injured?" he inquired disdainfully. "We don't need babies here." Donté's morale was broken, but he assumed his characteristic stoicism and pushed forward. By the end of November, as football season drew to a close, he made a notable catch that caught everyone's attention. Beaming, he shared the news with Don over the phone, evoking the biggest smiles and words of praise from his father.

Lurking in the back of his mind, the following must have haunted him.

Radiant_memes: "You can't go wrong with suicide. It solves everything."

Dont'e to zodiak.killer: "[I'd] jump off a really high building or shoot myself. Probley only reason I haven't done it yet is there are no really high buildings where I live and I got no gunz."

In Two Universes

What degradation of our son! What he must have been holding inside! How horrible and unthinkable! Most likely, he thought that we would never believe what was happening to his psyche and what precipitated his descent into utter chaos *at the mere prompting of thugs*. His helplessness whirled out of control, with nowhere to turn, he thought. He was torn between two universes—one filled with light, the other with shadow, vacillating between success and humiliation by those who should have served as examples. One look, one word of reassurance from the proper sources (i.e., adolescent psychologists and other support staff within the high school) would have made a difference—or perhaps, *no* words, but rather, overt support from a trained professional to whom he could have reached out on the school's premises. Instead, our fourteen-year-old stood senselessly on the precipice of uncertainty, confusion, and *the end*.

Thanksgiving Homecoming, 2016

Don came home in November to spend four days over the holidays in Maine. Dont'e was ready to display his solid first-quarter report card grades, and Don was very pleased. The taste of freedom did not seem to be wasted on our son who, we firmly believed, was thriving. Don shared his love of hiking in the mountains of Utah and offered to take Dont'e with him during that summer, in addition to going skydiving at our adventurous boy's request.

Don returned to Utah in a refreshed state of mind, intending to come back home for Christmas. Meanwhile, Dont'e and Kelly resumed their daily routine, with the inclusion of a geometry tutor to improve his grades and exam results.

A Highly Unusual Request, Christmas, 2016

Before we knew it, Christmas lights glistened in the windows, and the air was filled with a cold that defied description. Don returned again for a brief three-day hiatus with his family, enjoyed a promised movie with Dont'e, and categorically denied his unusual request to purchase a caliber weapon (something we would *never* allow in our home). Dont'e always had been a conservative actor, never asking for much of anything for himself. In hindsight, his request for a lethal weapon appeared to be out of character, but we had so much faith and trust in him that when we said "no," we knew that would put an end to the matter—and it did—until later when we recovered a post to the effect that "I would have used a gun to kill myself, but I didn't because I thought it would make my parents sad."

Sweet, Fleeting Mundaneness.

During Maine's winter months, activities slackened, but Dont'e and Kelly maintained their routine, uneventful, but steady, having fun with their first-time use of the snowblowers, Dont'e Chinese dinner with friends, attendance at birthday parties, and an occasional movie when the wind and snow did not lift them into another stratosphere. One evening, Dont'e attended a sleepover at Peter Blackwell's house. He was Gabe Higgin's friend, and Kelly had no cause for alarm. They were buddies—children with whom our son was familiar and spent time in the past.

The phone would ring. "Hey, Dad! Everything's fine!" However, something very sinister was in progress, threatening to rob us of the love of our life and every joy that we had ever known.

Early Memories, Especially With Cousin Sara

Dont'e and Cousin Sara

CHAPTER 8

EXTINGUISHED LIGHT

(Kelly's Narrative)

Attentive, loving mothers never take one moment with their children for granted. With Dont'e, it was easy to savor every moment. The 'ordinary days' always had something remarkable about them—however seemingly inconsequential—a look, a smile, a glass of my son's much-loved milk in hand. With us, nothing went unnoticed.

Sunday, March 5, 2017 was no exception. We watched a movie and I made a typical salmon and salad dinner for us. The fact that Don was away in Utah clouded our joy a little, but we were in touch, and all was well. Dont'e asked me to make brownies (his favorite), and later, we prepared for the beginning of the week. Except for the fact that Dont'e had not hit the 'send' button on his homework assignment, absolutely nothing seemed out of sync. His grades in math and history had declined a little, but I wasn't that concerned. A tutor's intervention always fixed the issue.

Nonetheless, when I saw that his laptop was open, with his homework still on the screen, I became stern. "What's this? Why haven't you sent in your homework?" I wanted to know.

Dont'e just shrugged his shoulders and kept silent. His demeanor was slightly odd and uncharacteristically aloof, but what fifteen-year-old adolescent boy doesn't have his moods?

"Are you smoking something? What is going on with you?" I pressed, in an adamant tone.

Dont'e grinned and shrugged off my question again. "I don't have to take a test tomorrow," he replied casually.

I looked at the screen and saw that he had blocked someone. Unbeknownst to me at the time, that single act was a red flag. Someone was harassing my son, and I did not know it. To this day, I'm filled with guilt for not probing further, but given our close relationship, I believed, with every breath, that Dont'e would confide in me if he felt the need. I never imagined that silence was consuming him from within—an anguish so deep that he could not reach out to his mother who would hang the moon for him, if I could.

March 6, 2017, the next morning. I awakened my son, as usual, at 6:00 a.m., and everything proceeded like clockwork. He had breakfast, and slid by me playfully, as I stood at the kitchen counter, with a brownie in his hand.

"What? You're eating a brownie at this time in the morning?"

"Come on, Mom, please!" he joked, peering out from the bathroom door.

Dont'e then headed into the shower, and when he finished, we talked about the day. "I lost my debit card, and I have to go to the bank after work. Do you want me to pick you up after work, or should I just meet you at home?" I asked.

"Meet me at home," my son replied.

I did not observe any changes in his demeanor. He simply appeared prepared for an ordinary day, with his backpack at the door and his sneakers ready for use. However, nothing about that day was routine.

I left for work around 7:45 a.m., expecting the bus to pick him up 15 minutes later. I trusted that Dont'e would be on time, as he had only been late once. At the time, he had fallen asleep on the couch and ended up walking to school.

At 10:00 a.m., I received a call from the school secretary. "Dont'e did not show up for second period," she said.

Perplexed, I asked, "was he in first period?"

"I have to ask the guidance counselor," the secretary replied, placing me on hold.

Soon, she returned and stated, "He wasn't in first period either."

I disconnected the call and immediately phoned my son. When I did not receive a response, I texted him, with the same result. I then left work and drove home to find Donté's backpack and sneakers in the same place as when I left. I fought a deep-seated, sinking feeling in my stomach. *My son has been kidnapped!* I thought, running from room to room, calling his name, "Dont'e!"

Seized with panic, I called the police department. "Please come right away! My son is missing." I was too numb to cry, feeling that I might burst from the gripping emotions welling within me.

When the first officer came to the door, I repeated that I could not find Dont'e.

"Would you mind if I look around?" the officer inquired.

"No, I don't mind," I said, trying to maintain composure.

We searched the house and went down to the basement where my son's bedroom was. He was not there. At first, it hadn't dawned on me to check the other side of the basement, since only a small storage area and an oil tank occupied that space. On second thought, however, I decided to look there and found my son in a standing position, seemingly looking at the floor.

At first glance, I didn't realize what was before me—my son's lifeless form—and I began to say, "Dont'e, what are you doing here?" Then, I noticed the rope around his neck. Beneath the rope was a shirt, tied around his neck, over which the rope was draped. I screamed and fell to the floor, releasing my bladder's contents. In an effort to help him to breathe, I rose, instinctively grabbed my son, and tried to hold him up. The officer assisted in my effort, at first, but then pulled me away. "He's cold," he said.

So was I. I didn't know what I felt, except that perhaps I had died. My soul's light was extinguished, and I was helpless. There would be no morning sun or evening moon in my world. Everything turned dark and empty, and I was left alone to wonder why.

The search for reasons and answers would be as agonizing as the tragedy itself. Only later did Don and I find our son's suicide note, written on the notepad of his smartphone, which read,

"I'm sorry you had to find this, but I can't take it anymore. No, it's not the grades or what will happen, but it's what kind of edged me off. I love you both, Mom and Dad." The police failed to discover this piece of evidence, even though the phone had been at the police station for nearly two weeks. In the three years since Donté's departure, we have had an opportunity to reflect with each passing moment. In the process of agonizing and ruminating, life's clues—and Dont'e himself—have provided startling answers. Not everything is as it appears on the face of things, and we couldn't just walk away and accept what had happened to us.

Strength is derived from the power of knowledge, action, and revelation, and Don and I resolved never to be silent. Donté's legacy is the truth—evidenced by words spoken and unspoken, evil deeds and doers that lurked silently in the background of our lives, finding tragic, horrific expression in the extinguishment of our life's greatest light.

CHAPTER 9

IN ANOTHER WORLD

(Don's narrative)

I have seen the world from various angles and perspectives, and I have always considered myself to be a citizen of the universe, capable of being anywhere, at any time, rising to every occasion—come what may.

Since I was a young boy, I always knew that I would serve my country. I never shied away from a challenge—even when learning the complex syntax of the German language, for which I received a Certificate of Training in 1986, at the age of twenty-three.

While in the Army, serving in Europe, I lived in East and West Germany and took in the rich cultural diversity of various countries while serving on the frontier of freedom in Berlin during the Cold War. In November 1989, I manned the Berlin Wall and witnessed its collapse and the reunification of families and friends after almost three decades' separation. That night, thousands of East Germans rushed to the barrier and demanded that the gates be opened. Never could I have imagined, in those riveting moments that, in my own lifetime, a barrier to the precious soul I loved most would be permanently edified.

My time in the military was intense and often unnerving. I received numerous Army achievement medals and commendations, always with my feet firmly planted on the ground, never flinching in fear or hesitation.

Then, on March 6, 2017, the battle of my lifetime ominously confronted me. There were no trenches in which to hide, no refuge from the cruel enemy that broke me at the seams, tore at my sinews, and threatened to snuff out every small gasp of air.

My on-the-job training in Salt Lake City, Utah, had been going well, and I had established a good rapport with neighbors, particularly my landlady, who showed me enormous kindness during my adjustment period. My living arrangements were comfortable, and I was, in most respects, settled in for my six-month training sessions. In my off hours, I enjoyed hiking in Utah's spectacular mountains, sometimes venturing off the beaten path where I encountered breathtaking views, which I could not wait to share with my son.

Monday, March 6, 2017 was, by all accounts, an ordinary, brisk day. In the morning, I received a call from Kelly, whose voice escalated to a panic level during the call. "The school's secretary called and said that Dont'e didn't show up for the first or second period," she said, trying to catch her breath. "I returned home from work, and I cannot locate Dont'e anywhere. He doesn't answer my calls and texts, and I've called the police."

I froze, and my intuition told me that something had gone horribly wrong. At about 10:35 a.m., the Bangor police arrived at our home. Minute by minute, I called and texted Kelly without receiving any replies. I began to experience severe anxiety, relentless stomach-churning, and I feared the worst. I then initiated calls to the Bangor Police Department, hoping to receive news from an officer on the scene.

"We're sending the local Utah police to come and speak with you," an officer informed me.

I fell to my knees, sobbing uncontrollably. Never could I have believed that my son would have initiated self-induced asphyxiation—a boy of unparalleled kindness and caring, with an extraordinary ability to remain calm in virtually every situation— an individual who never once in his life exhibited anger, resentment, or disrespect and was never in trouble with the law.

Notwithstanding my convictions, everything that I thought I knew with certainty was about to change, and I would be transported into another world. During my forty-five minute wait for news, my delirious mind played back random scenes from our recent past, like an old movie reel, where my son dwelled and shared his life with us. There he was, playing with his favorite cousin, Sara, at Halloween, sitting in Santa's lap at the mall, muddying his hands in the spring grass, shooting Roman candles with his friend, Sam.

There he was, a mere child, writing me an illustrated letter, pleading with me to stop smoking, telling me of the certain dangers to my life if I continued. (from that day on, I never touched another cigarette, even in the depths of my grief.) There he was, in my office, conversing with me, running around in our yard, playing with friends, being silly with Mom, frolicking with a dolphin on our Caribbean cruise, bonding with me in Cape Coral, Florida, situating Stewie on top of his head for the ride of that lizard's life. There he was, feeding the ducks at lunchtime, ambling into the kitchen, with his signature glass of milk, commenting to his best friend, "You know, I'd marry a cow, if I could. I love milk that much!" he would say—and he meant it. There he was, barely on the threshold of manhood, wearing his football jersey, number 42, looking like an Adonis (of the most humble, unassuming kind).

Never would I see all the memorable events that could have taken place in his life. Never again could I lavish him with surprises, like a painball park on the twenty eight acres of land I had purchased. (Shortly before his passing, we had discussed this project, and I had planned to surprise him with it upon his high school graduation). Now, I only could envision the joy. My mind raced.

When the terrible, most tragic moment of truth arrived, I had been pacing, unable to control my thoughts or calm my racing heart. Two officers approached, with pained expressions. "Your son has ended his life," one of them solemnly told me. I fell to the asphalt, hardly able to breathe. Once I returned to the apartment, I hyperventilated profusely and had to breathe into a paper bag. I wanted to die and hoped to have a heart attack, but somehow, I managed to restore some level of composure—just enough to call my landlady. She was instrumental in arranging for a flight and bereavement fare out of Utah that evening.

During the day, neighbors remained at my side and tried to comfort me. Though I was very grateful for their support, all I remember was my pervasive stupor. Later, I boarded my flight and learned that there were two connecting flights out of Utah. Due to my state of mind at the time, I cannot remember the stops. I do, however, recall experiencing hysteria just before the second plane took off and being escorted off the plane and into the terminal. There, I waited for about four to five hours before boarding my last flight to Bangor.

Upon my arrival, I somehow mustered the fortitude to call my sister-in-law, who met me at the airport and drove me home. Like everyone who knew Dont'e, she was beside herself in shock. Kelly was waiting for me at home with her two sisters, Cathy and Tracey, and her brother, Daniel. Earlier, her best friend had come to remain with her after the tragic event.

Our great support systems notwithstanding, both of us were nonfunctional. Darkness turned into daylight … and then, again … and again … The world continued to spin on its axis, as we wondered how and why, when everything we knew had come to a precipitous, nightmarish end.

CHAPTER 10

THE REALM OF 'IF ONLY'

The Final Goodbye, March 7-12, 2017

The days following Donté's death were a complete blur. We just went through the motions of breathing and wondering how we would navigate from one moment to the next. Preparing for a wake and funeral for the love of our life was the most horrible process that any two individuals could face. Parents never expect to bury their child—a part of their soul—an expression of their love and legacy in the world. To have to part with so much hope and to writhe in what 'could-have-been' was unthinkable.

We agonized in the realm of "if only." *If only* the call center employees had done their jobs, *if only* the school administration had assumed accountability for the malevolent acts of hatred on their premises and taken action to excoriate the perpetrators, *if only* Dont'e had chosen not to suffer in silence (one second was too long!), *if only* he had confided in us and revealed the contents of his precious heart! *If only* … It was all too much. We were going through the fires of the inferno, without an exit strategy. Admittedly, we questioned the purpose of our own existence. We now realize that we were not alone in our extreme grief. Tragically, there are many parents who experience such emotions, especially when the system breaks down, as in Donté's case, and fails to provide a rescue for the heaviest of hearts. The pain was unspeakable—as it still is, to this day—and always will remain. The grief only augments with time, matched solely by the rage and incredulity that pervaded every fiber of our being. We slept a lot, and allowed days to transition into nights, without paying the cyclical process any mind at all. Thankfully, we had family and friends to assist with the preparations, but mostly, we were on autopilot, living for our son.

To compound matters, we became aware, after visiting the funeral home, that protocol was not followed in the last stages of Donté's earthly journey. When Don went to the funeral home to recover our son's personal effects, he discovered, to his horror, that they had been discarded, due to their "soiled" condition. That act added to our emotional distress and sense of loss, as we recognized that yet another injustice had been meted upon our family. Don found himself engaged in advocacy in the depths of grief, which made the process of paying final homage to our son even more difficult. Once he pointed out the egregious wrong-doing, the funeral home director had no choice but to compensate us for the mishandling of our son's clothes.

Later, an expert funeral director out of state corroborated the misdeed and confirmed that all clothes and other personal property must travel with the deceased to the coroner's office. Once the death certificate is issued and the deceased is transferred to the funeral home, those in possession of the property must consult with the next of kin and schedule a conference to determine whether the property should be returned or tossed away. Instead of receiving the requisite counseling, we were dismissed as though we were statistics, heaped upon a dustbin of others in our circumstances.

Lives are consequential. Flesh and bone, spirit and heart must be honored at all times. What were so-called Bangor industry professionals thinking? *Oh, this was just another teen suicide, just another kid, just another set of grieving parents.* No! Life and death are endemic to the human condition, no doubt, but nothing about the cycle is routine.

Yet, going through the motions seems to be a way of life in insular communities. The police investigative report documenting Donté's death almost reads like a to-do list. In rote fashion, the sergeant on duty wrote:

Decedent LSA @ approx.. 6:30 this a.m. Decedent's mother woke him up to get ready for school as she always does. He got up, did his normal routine. Mom leaves for work at 6:45 a.m., and decedent usually boards the bus at

7:15 a.m. Mom received a call from the school stating that decedent did not show up for school. Mom went back home and could not find the decedent. Decedent has a bedroom in the basement. He is found around a corner where there is a storage area. He has used a thin rope which is fastened to an outside electrical line. No concerns for electrocution. He stood on a chair and stepped off. One leg is through the back of the chair, and the other knee on the floor. Nothing suspicious was noted. Decedent's mother stated that the decedent has not been acting abnormal at all, she knows of nothing in his life that was going on that would lead him to take his own life. He is in the ROTC program at school and is a good student. No notes have been found at this time.

Job done, mission accomplished, case closed. The sergeant simply took the the event at face value and considered it to be an open and shut case, without any further probing. He did not even look at Donté's phone, where we later found the suicide note. The sergeant performed a light dusting of the window sills around Dont'e, without more, and left. He neither referred to the fact that there were multiple failed attempts (judging by the ceiling's condition) nor the presence of the shirt tied around our son's neck. Why did Dont'e resort to that measure? Typically, suicides are not performed with the use of a shirt and a rope. A suicidal person does not contemplate the means of execution with such exactitude.

"I'd love if it someone killed me though," I later read in a social media post. Was this an actual suicide or an act fa-

cilitated by someone else? The question remains open and perhaps we never will know the answer.

As we later found out, the rope was discarded. A follow-up with a valid search warrant did not enter the conversation. The fact that, in plain view, "nothing suspicious was noted" was sufficient in the minds of law enforcement—in keeping with Bangor's clichéd, topical society. What you see is what you get.

Our son had ended his life, and so concluded the inquiry. The fact that Dont'e did not fit the risk profile and that all appeared normal prior to the events that led to his demise meant nothing to the police. Law enforcement was dutiful and did what they had to do under the circumstances— but was that *really* the case? We emphatically pose the question, "Should there ever be such an incident as 'a routine suicide?'

No reasonable person can answer affirmatively. There had to have been *something* that was overlooked. For example, we do not have DNA evidence to prove any conclusive findings that Dont'e handled the rope that was discarded, as were his clothes. By all appearances, he died by self-asphyxiation, but surface appearances alone do not always tell the whole story. On its face, the case seemed to be a suicide, but further investigation should have taken place, along with the mechanistic protocol. How can anyone conclusively establish what occurred without a thorough investigation, ruling out other possibilities? Blood evidence was not found at the scene in plain sight, but what about latent evidence—in the floorboards or in other rooms of the house? No one set foot there to look at any time. Law enforcement confined the search to the narrow zone of the storage area and drew a conclusion (or, rather, a *mere inference*).

As parents, we deserved more than just a slip of paper parroting facts—as does anyone who has had a such a devastating loss. "It's not my job, there is no time to conduct further investigations, I acted according to established practices," some might say. But lives are not routine and in death, answers must follow. *If only . . .*

Such were the thoughts that whirled in our minds as we prepared for the final goodbye. At the wake, all of our sons' JROTC buddies huddled in a circle, held each other, and cried. They were clearly grieving, too —that valiant group of boys, barely having lived, facing the privy thief of death claim their good friend. It was heartbreaking to see. We don't know how the school dealt with the issue or whether they did so with any kind of heart or insight. Judging by the way subsequent suicides were handled (over an intercom system), it is unlikely that anyone proactively intervened on a one-to-one basis.

One incident at the wake stood out to us: Peter Blackwell stood near Donté's coffin, like a sentinel, throughout the entire day and night, not moving an inch. People came and went, and there was Peter, immovable and expressionless,standing beside the coffin, as though he were guarding over our son—in an eerie manner. At the time, we were too immersed in our grief to notice him, but in hindsight, we found his behavior quite strange and troubling. It seemed as though he were physically expressing his post, though body language: "[You see,] you can't go wrong with suicide. It solves everything."

In a very real sense, Peter had 'won.' He had assumed dominion and control over Donté's life, only to witness him following suit and acquiescing in the evil scheme. In those moments (we should say *hours*), the bully seemed to claim his prize. He didn't have to say a word to speak volumes.

Other students were complicit in the scheme, as well. We don't doubt that some felt intense regret, including his best friend, GH, and other JROTC members who truly bonded with him. We don't purport to understand what any of them were going through or to fathom the extent of the emotional scars that some undoubtedly experienced. However, it is telling that someone knew exactly what was happening to Dont'e, but stood by, in a state of inertia, without uttering a word.

Oddly, several days after the wake, we received an anonymous telephone call from a girl, sobbing uncontrollably, "I'm so sorry, I'm so sorry!" The girl sounded as if she had reached the end of her rope, and we feared for her safety. When we attempted to call her back, another unknown voice answered. When we asked for the original girl, the call recipient said, "I don't know her. She just borrowed my phone."

Another telling omission came into view: Three of Donté's teachers chose not to attend the wake and subsequently have not expressed condolences for his loss. The principal attempted to justify their snub by saying that everyone grieves differently; but not to appear at all or offer any expressions of sorrow is a negation of human compassion—a pervasive failure, symptomatic of the community (with some exceptions).

The significance of these incidents may not seem readily apparent, but the events demonstrate that knowledge existed among Donte's peer group, without a single offer of enlightenment. We literally remained in the dark, without a lighthouse anywhere in view.

Not until two months later, when Don went on his "crusade," did we unearth the abject evil that prompted our son to leave the world.

CHAPTER 11

THE CRUSADE

The days following the funeral were surreal. The music of laughter and the bustle of movement ceased, and we wondered how we would go on. The trauma of finding our son left Kelly in a stupor, disinclined to do anything but weep. We spoke infrequently and just tried to breathe . . . from one moment to the next.

Along with the indescribable grief, Don was seething inside. He had a complete meltdown and was determined to get to the core of the question, *"How could a child like our son, filled with love and a grounded sense of self, leave the world by his own hand?"* Nothing made sense.

Somehow, we managed to pick ourselves up and fly to Utah to retrieve Don's car and other belongings and close out his commitments there. We traveled three hundred miles a day, stopping to rest in the late afternoons.

On the way, we toured the southeastern seaboard, stopping in Florida to revisit some of the places we had been as a family. The beaches, the storefronts, the skylines, the sun, and moon—everything reminded us of our son. We saw his face and felt his presence everywhere, regretting that he did not stay in the Sunshine State, where he and Stewie had thrived so well. We could never have imagined that returning to Maine would be the death knell of life as we knew it. If only Dont'e had said the word, we would have gone back in a minute, but we cannot speculate on what *could have been.*

In the evenings, while staying with friends, Don sat at his computer, trying to accumulate as much information on suicides as possible, leaving no stone unturned.

Feeling overwhelmed and broken, Kelly decided to fly home, and Don remained and drove back to Maine alone. His blood simmered in his veins. Whatever happens to their child, parents have visceral feelings about their fate. Our son was just a boy, innocent, unassuming, and pressures continued to mount. Dont'e believed in human goodness, and when he discovered that not everyone has noble intentions, he buckled. Then, observing his inner turmoil, he intelligently and soulfully reached out to the crisis call center.

Hi, I'm Dont'e Izzo. I'm thinking of killing myself. My depression and stuff [are] building up really hard. I feel that I've just been taking up space for the last half year.

I'm thinking of a plan of killing myself, including hanging if I obtain no gun soon. The only reason I haven't done it yet is because I don't want my parents to be sad.

Donté's second call consisted of the following dialogue:
"How are you doing now?"

"I'm okay."

Such brevity is enough to explain the complete dismissiveness and inaction of those charged with saving adolescents. Look at the equation: No follow-through + failure to notify parents + dismissiveness + just-a-day-at-the-office-mentality = DEATH.

On the way back to Maine, Don felt enraged and called Gabe to ask about Peter. As he was on the road, Don received a call from an unsympathetic Peter, who did not admit to anything—neither his communications with our son nor the incendiary posts.

"You have two ways to go," Don admonished him. "Either stand up and admit the truth, or I'll tell your parents."

"I'm suicidal, too, and I'm going to blame you," Peter defiantly asserted. Anyway, my Dad said that I shouldn't speak to you anymore."

Don was fuming. About three months after the tragedy, he went to a data recovery center with Donté's two phones and found the communications that alerted us to the types of people with whom Dont'e had been associating: white supremacists, narcissists, and hate-mongers, who encouraged him to take his own life.

Whenever and wherever we could, we reached out to those we thought were friends, and even made a lunch appointment with Peter Blackwell's parents. They were evasive, in denial, and deflected from the truth, insinuating ignorance on their son Peter's part. We had reason to believe that his odious ideology stemmed from home. How else could a child develop a hate-based mindset? Children are blank slates, and they emulate what they see and hear in their home environments. Parents, therefore, have the paramount responsibility of socializing their children to respect their peers and others. Without that ethic, we have a clueless, licentious society.

Soon after that meeting, Don approached two of Donté's peers sitting on a park bench. They were the individuals who had invited Dont'e to a group chat but ignored him the whole time. Both were extremely arrogant and condescending and admitted that they had dismissed our son. Then, they ran home and called the police, and before we knew what was happening, two officers came to our door with a no-contact order, and the kids refused to answer any more of Don's questions. A grieving father was simply seeking answers—some indications of what could have led to our son's tragic demise, but everyone was clandestine and detached.

The pain of the deplorable treatment was compounded by the fact that Donté's peers had been his friends since elementary school. Over time, we socialized with and felt close to them. Instead of coming to our side, however, they shunned us and abnegated their responsibilities as teachers and leaders in the community. They were too busy saving face and downplayed the death of an innocent child. One of the mothers described the racist posts to Kelly as "just boy talk."

Silence and inaction are tantamount to complicity in an unjust outcome. People cannot just stand by and allow teen suicides to take place without saying or doing anything to end the cycle of despair.

Our situation is not unique. Everything is rooted in cause-and-effect scenarios. If society does not take an interest and views suicides as routine or a 'hush-hush' topic, to be ignored and swept under the rug, how can we, as parents, ever expect to take preemptive action against such tragedies?

As much as we tried to reach out, our inquiries fell on deaf ears. Even when communicating with the school superintendent, Betsy Webb we could not find answers. That official was, essentially, silent, detached, and unconcerned by the urgency of our pleas. It was not until Kelly wrote to her, appealing to her as a mother for a response, did she take steps to reply.

On more than one occasion, Don attempted to reach out to the Bangor Deputy Chief and was referred to Superintendent Webb and back again. We felt as though we were in an endless tennis match. Sadly, no enlightenment came.

The following series of email communications, between Kelly and Superintendent Betsy Webb (nearly two years after our son's passing), illustrates our futile quest for answers. Our son was a target, at the mercy of peer cruelty and taunting. We knew of the white supremacists' hand in his pain, but there were others, as well (Note Kelly's reference to another student, "ZW," who allegedly used a pejorative toward Dont'e and pushed him in the locker room. However, the student who initially gave us this information later recanted, citing a mistaken belief. We were constantly in the dark.)

Wed, Jan 31, 2018 at 3:54 PM, Kelly Izzo wrote:

Mrs. Webb, my husband had a lengthy conversation with Deputy Chief Bushey at the Bangor Police Dept., as you instructed us to do. Deputy Chief Bushey stated that our questions and concerns need to be addressed by you, the Superintendent of Schools. He said he would reach out to Mr. B (Principal) because he feels for our concerns, questions and frustrations that are not being addressed. So here we are again, back at the school department. Were do we go from here, Mrs. Webb?

On Thu, Feb 1, 2018 at 1:15 PM, Bangor Supt. wrote:

Mrs. Izzo,

I spoke with Deputy Chief Bushey and he shared your husband has questions about School Department policy. Mr. B (Principal) and I would be happy to meet with him to answer his questions. Please share some dates and times that would work for him and I will schedule an appointment.

Sincerely,

Betsy Webb

On Thu, Feb 1, 2018 at 1:44 PM, Kelly Izzo wrote:

Are we talking about my husband meeting with you and Mr. B (Principal)?

On Fri, Feb 2, 2018 at 2:20 PM, Kelly Izzo wrote:

?

On Sun, Feb 4, 2018 at 12:37 PM, Bangor Supt. wrote:

Yes. If a phone call is preferred, let me know.

On Mon, Feb 5, 2018 at 7:24 PM, Kelly Izzo wrote:

How about I just state the questions and concerns again and you provide me the answers?

Why and how do the circumstances between Dont'e and ZW and their encounter, "warrant camaraderie." We have a communication transpired between ZW and Dont'e at a school dance in which ZW refers to Dont'e as "F--kboi." We also have a statement from an individual of contact from ZW toward Dont'e in the school locker room.

More important is the reference by from two school officials, Mr. B (Principal) and Mr. HM that "camaraderie" is a justification of contact between my son and ZW. (In addition, other behaviors by this student show a pattern of indifference.) I would like to know the rationale.

Why did the Cyr school bus driver completely fail to stop for my son at our house for school pick up on TWO occasions in the same month?

There was not one inquiry made to us or my son, explaining the major letter-grade drops in most of his classes. Two letter-grade plummets in two classes. History and Geometry. (This should have been addressed before the end of the 1st quarter, either with my son, his parents, or all of us.)

On Tue, Feb 6, 2018 at 9:02 AM, Bangor Supt. Betsy Webb wrote:

We would like to meet with you to address these questions. Please let me know dates and times that work for you.

Sincerely,

Betsy Webb

On Thu, Feb 8, 2018 at 11:45 AM, Kelly Izzo wrote:

Presently, we are not in Maine and this would create a burden for us.

On Mon, Feb 12, 2018 at 6:24 PM, Kelly Izzo wrote to Supt. Betsy Webb:

Do you plan on answering?

Complete silence ensued, and once again, a follow-up and follow-through were non-existent.

As to the bullying incidents, our entreaties for clarification were met with denial after denial, and even Donté's purported best friend turned the other way. "That kid wasn't bullied. I would have known about it," Gabe Higgins declared.

Who refers to his deceased best friend as "that kid" in such a cavalier manner?

And what about the other students? No one can tell us, to this day, with any degree of sincerity, that they knew nothing. Although we are mindful of the fact that their young minds were impressionable and that, no doubt, they were trying to process what had happened to our son, virtually no one deigned to say that outright or *anything* to provide solace in our hour of despair.

Recently, we learned that Superintendent Webb is stepping down from her position in October 2020 and is scheduled to spearhead a university program designed to raise awareness about systemic racism and how to prevent its spread. The irony of this latest development cannot be overstated, particularly given the consistent pattern of racist/supremacist conduct that has taken place on her watch over the course of many years. Moreover, in the last two years, Don repeatedly has attempted to reach out to Superintendent Webb to decry Bangor High School's practices of evasion on the race issue, without any response.

Recently, five black indigenous students of color have stepped forward with complaints of harassment and discrimination—to no avail. The deplorable treatment of these individuals is akin to the racism perpetuated in the Antebellum South. Yet, no one in the school administration has taken any action to bring the endemic problem to light or ameliorate their suffering. The students' extraordinary courage in speaking out, however, has brought their unequal treatment to the fore of the school administration's consciousness and has launched a new movement that focuses on the enlightenment of faculty, staff, and fellow students.

The high school loves to tout its numbers and show how much ahead of the nationwide academic curve students are. Although numbers are indicative of performance, they do not supplant humanity or accountability. An exclusionary culture pervades the school environment, and if the masses cannot attest to that, it is because 'the masses' have no idea about what it means to be marginalized.

Like the students of color and others who have been forced into silence—either by fear, intimidation, or apathy—our son was subjugated by an ideology of exclusion. Everyone knew about it. Supremacist rhetoric and action had the floor while everyone turned the other way.

Yet, still now, as Donté's peers approach the age of nineteen and are full adults, they are strangely noncommittal. All attempts to reach out to Gabe and his family (to whom we were once extremely close) has evoked a disturbing silence. Not having answers is almost as tortuous as losing Dont'e. We therefore urge anyone who knows anything to come forward. From our grieving hearts, we would be forever grateful.

In those first days, grasping at straws, trying to breathe from one moment to the next, we stopped at nothing, but our efforts were futile. Although our appeal to Senator Angus King yielded a courteous reply, he was unable to intervene, as we had moved to Florida by then and were no longer Maine residents. Below is the substance of Don's communication and the senator's reply:

Dear Senator King:

First, allow me, as a father and a disabled veteran, to describe my son's temperament, character, kindness, and overall personality. My son was a very gentle boy with the fantastic ability of calmness. Never once did I ever see him get angry! Never once had my son ever shown any frowns, curled lips, faces of discontent, or disrespect. He never was in any trouble with the law. He made the honor roll from 2012-2015 in two states, and mostly maintained a GPA of 3.0 from 1st grade to high school freshman year. He played football from the time of second grade to 2016. He ran cross country, participated in JROTC, and was a reputable young man.

I have tried in vain to seek justice and answers in his name, through fluctuating emotions—from deep sadness to outright anger. I have gone to the local police, the Attorney General, and the school department—all to no avail!

My son, Dont' e Izzo, took his own life on March 6, 2017. He was bullied, and I have factual information in my possession, which points to that. He also was conversing with peers about taking his life, and the peer (with whom we are acquainted) suggested suicide to him and told him that suicide would be his best option, and he couldn't go wrong with suicide. Also, the principle and the JV football coach ruled that an incident with a fellow football player in which the individual chest-shoved my child and berated him for not playing hard enough was "camaraderie!" How can that type of conduct be deemed "camaraderie?"

Also, my son carried a 3.0 GPA from 1st grade all the way to the 1st quarter of tenth grade, then dropped two letter grades in two classes and one letter grade in other classes. No one at the school said a word.

I have shared all my complaints with school officials who have run me into the ground with prejudice and passive resistance. They refuse to make an inquiry to establish whether or not my son was bullied. It is bizarre that nobody wants to know. Never in all my life have I been presented with such discord and disrespect!

Thank you for your time and attention.

Sincerely,

Don Izzo

Dear Mr. Izzo

Thank you for contacting me,
I really appreciate the opportunity to hear what's on your mind.

I would like to share with you that it is a longstanding courtesy between members of Congress that each elected official be allowed to exclusively address his or her own constituents' questions, concerns and requests.

When you sent me your message, you indicated an address outside of Maine. If you are not a resident of Maine, I encourage you contact your own United States Senators. They are in a much better position to assist you. As I do for Maine, your own Senators better know the resources, issues and data that are pertinent to your message and home state. Given the volume of correspondence that I receive, I am only able to respond to Mainers.

Again, thank you for writing to me.

Best regards,

Senator Angus S. King, Jr.

We appreciate Senator King's kindness.

As the days passed, our plight was not squarely confronted with compassion or proactivity by anyone in authority with the power to act, despite our pleas. Adrift on an ocean without a life raft, we were at the mercy of those wielding the mighty swords of status, labels, and titles by which they were defined. Yet, the humanitarian intentions that should and must underlie the letters next to their names were sorely lacking.

Beleaguered by the gnawing urge to pursue justice in our son's name, we continued our crusade, and then, one day, another tsunami hit and carried us away.

CHAPTER 12

A SECOND WAVE

As any parent who has lost a child knows all too well, the cliché, "time heals all wounds," could not be more trite or painful. Sands slowly pour into the proverbial hourglass as day turns into night without your knowledge. You walk on shaky ground, barely breathe, make meager attempts to eat and sleep, but these movements and habits become rote, without meaning or substance. Your faith becomes tenuous, and you wonder why you are here. You even question your identity. "Widows" and "widowers" have lost spouses; children who lose parents become "orphans," but what is the term for those who have lost children—the core and essence of ourselves? The term "childless parents" is a cruel oxymoron that seems to widen the excruciating, permanent hole in your heart.

So, what's left? *Action!* The first life-changing move was leaving our home in Bangor. The community we called home since Dont'e was a child was the same place that ultimately toppled the notions that we had infused in our son's mind and heart by its clandestine homogeneity—the desire to preserve cliques of convenience and power, along with the status quo. *Just another teen suicide. It happens all the time. We grieve, keep silent, and move on.* That stance is toxic and deadly.

Especially for Kelly, moving to Florida, where we spent many happy times as a family, was essential. The house in Maine held too many memories—and nightmares. So, we packed up and downsized to the utmost extent. Besides, material possessions meant nothing to us anymore. All that we ever had was gone.

However, one thing remained—as it does to this day—the urgency of 'why?', particularly with regard to the crisis call center's failure to follow through after Donté's calls for help. That realization compounded our sense of loss. *Our son's death could have been prevented*, and the call center's act of omission was nothing short of gross negligence.

In 2017, immediately upon our return to Bangor, after receiving the report from the data recovery service, we decided to bring an action against the call center. Don did not know where to seek legal counsel, but began his pursuit for representation. Many practitioners advised him to search within the Reno, Nevada area, the call center's location. Our cause was justice and maximum compensatory damages. We fully expected it, but we could not have anticipated the second wave of grief that subsumed our lives in waves of inequity.

It took Don about two weeks to find Craig Murphy, a prominent Nevada personal injury attorney, whose kindness we will never forget. Don spoke to him for over a week, and he listened and advised with the utmost professionalism and concern. He was the one ray of light in our abyss of hopelessness. Unfortunately, since our case was not within his scope of expertise, he referenced us to Skip Simpson, Esq., a member of the American Association of Suicidology's Board of Directors, and said that he would make inquiries. Mr. Murphy then presented a battery of questions through Skip.

When we completed the interrogatories, Skip declined to take our case, and we were heart-broken. His reasoning: fifty-one days had passed between Donté's first call to the center and his passing. The insurance company concurred. We wondered how the timeframe between our son's plea and the tragedy was relevant. There should not have been a statute of limitations in our case. Negligence does not diminish with the passage of a mere fifty-one days!

Then, Don began communicating with Bill Bradley, Esq,, who agreed to take our case, but Mr. Bradley was initially tentative. He said that he had to confer with a colleague to discuss whether or not a duty of care existed on the call center's part. This claim did not sound in logic!

During our personal investigations and communications with legal practitioners, we have learned that a duty of care arises in three instances:

(1) Where a reasonable person owes a duty of care not to subject another to foreseen harms by their actions or acts of omission (failures to act).

(2) Where a fiduciary confidential and/or other special relationship exists between the parties that trigger the duty.

(3) Where the duty arises by statute.

The call center's very existence is predicated on a duty of care to the young lives whom it was designated to protect. The call center representatives act in a fiduciary capacity, dealing with confidential life-and-death scenarios every day. *In other words, the duty of care is inherent in their job description.*

When we discovered that Dont'e had made *two* calls to the center, not just one (as we initially thought), we were incredulous. Don had a breakdown, and his health was at serious risk.

Mr. Bradley's Demand Letter, filed one year after the complaint, was highly inaccurate, mentioning that only one representative (instead of two) had received a call from Dont'e and failed to take proactive measures. Both lawyers concurred that the number of individuals involved in taking our son's call was irrelevant to the case. We vehemently disagreed. The issue at hand: our son's security and, ultimately, his life. Instead of taking a compassionate interest, as they were purportedly trained to do, both women offhandedly dismissed his cries for help. It bears repeating that our son would be alive today if either of the representatives followed through with calls and texts or had notified us, in any way, of Donté's state of mind. *No child should have to die as a result of 'just-a-day-at-the-office' complacency!*

The lawyers' apathy came to light when we learned that it took a full year to submit the Demand Letter.

On July 1, 2019, we traveled to Nevada, where we booked a hotel in preparation for mediation. In our vulnerable state, we were unaware of the lawyers' sleight-of-hand. Mr. Bradley told Don that the insurance company required him, before mediation, to submit to an independent medical examination (IME), which brought back painful memories from his childhood. At the time, Don did not have the necessary equilibrium and presence of mind to move forward with the exam, and he wanted to initiate the court's protection. However, our lawyers sabotaged the effort and failed to file the motion.

To submit to the examination, Don had to drive three and a half hours. Feeling physically exhausted, depleted, and at the end of his rope, he arrived and sat as he was grilled with questions. For a grieving father, not quite lucid or focused, the process was unspeakably oppressive, particularly given the style and length of questioning that brought him back to the deeply painful experiences of his past. He wondered how any of the questions were relevant to the case at hand, and in truth, not one of them was germane. It seemed that the whole procedure was orchestrated to break him down. When he expressed his frustrations to Mr. Bradley about the long-distance drive and the nature of the test, the lawyer replied, "it was designed that way."

The detriment of the interrogatories cannot be overstated, especially given Don's preexisting state of mind, but no one cared. Again, clandestine homogeneity held sway—the predominance of like-minded, similarly situated individuals, in the game solely for self-gain, completely lacking in compassion.

Unbelievably, the examiners found that Don's responses were inadequate and that he had not applied himself. So, he had to submit to questioning again, still journeying in his mind back to the most distressing times of his life — though not nearly equal to the events of March 6, 2017.

Finally, Mr. Bradley informed us that the court had ordered mediation, pending a ruling on the defense's summary judgment motion. We were not present for that decision and urged our lawyer to discourage the settlement option. Instead of advocating for us, however, both lawyers simply sat back and played a numbers game without speaking on our behalf.

Although the judge used his discretion in opting for mediation, *we did not have to settle*. We were forced to do so against our will. We desperately wanted an opportunity for our case to be heard on the merits and have our rightful day in court, but Mr. Bradley used fear tactics and colluded with the mediator, formerly Judge Jackie Glass, to discourage our pursuit of a trial.

In an email dated July 17, 2018, Skip told Don that one of the authors of Suicide Prevention, Policies, Procedures, Guidelines, and Protocols could not testify as an expert witness because he was a government employee. Further, he stated that "…the best way [the expert] could help [was to] make the defendant settle to avoid the awful publicity this lawsuit could bring."

Skip's statement patently corroborated our view that by demanding that we settle, instead of going to trial, our attorneys were not acting as our advocates. Instead, they were participating in the denial of our due process rights. Why would publicity be "awful," when the very purpose of the lawsuit was to shed light on the call center's negligence in taking proactive steps to save our son's life? How could it be "awful" to expose that fatal misstep? In our grief, we wanted to be change agents so that what happened to our son would not be allowed to recur—not ever again. In those hours of our deepest grief, our lawyers suppressed our ability to declare our truth before a court and have a jury of our peers decide whether or not we had a claim. Instead, we were consigned to mediation, forced to settle against our will.

It was clear to us that the discussions were slanted in favor of the powerful—those with the upper hand, with a reputation in the community. No one ever put emphasis on the issue of someone dropping the ball by never pursuing communication with our son or notifying us of his calls. The second call center representative went so far as to say that even when there is a follow-through, suicide is a foregone conclusion. In her words, "they [the callers] do it anyway."

We were so beside ourselves that at one point, during a break from our mediation session, Don insisted that he did not want to proceed further or accept a settlement offer. At that point, Mr. Bradley grabbed him by the shoulders and said, "Don, if you don't take this offer, we will drop you as a client."

Naturally, Don was deeply upset and taken aback. Threats and intimidation had no place in that room—or anywhere. "Please remove your hands from my shoulders," Don insisted, rebelling against the attack on his person and dignity. Later, in an email communication, Mr. Bradley apologized for his conduct, but contrition did not take away from his unethical conduct.

All we wanted was a verdict that established a causal connection between our son's death and the call center's negligence—nothing more. Instead, we were coerced into a settlement from all angles—and to compound matters, Don sustained a battery—nonconsensual physically aggressive conduct.

A couple of rooms over, Kelly sat in conversation with Judge Glass, the mediator, who told her that we did not have a case, and if we did, the jury would not 'like' Don, and we would not receive a cent. The mediator further stated that if summary judgment was denied, or if we proceeded to trial and lost, the case would set a precedent, and no one could ever sue the call center again.

This tripartite assessment was flawed in numerous ways. First, the mediator erred and crossed a line by discussing a possible ruling on the merits of our case. She did not merely discuss the risks of going to trial and advise us with insight and empathy. Instead, her language placed us under duress. She wanted us to accept the settlement offer or suffer unfavorable consequences.

"When both sides are unhappy, that's a good day for the court," she declared. "You have the facts, they [meaning the other side] have the law." Such an assessment brought Kelly to tears.

Secondly, by making a value judgment about Don, the mediator violated her position of neutrality. She evidently forgot that we were in pain to begin with and poured acid on an open wound.

Third, the assertion that our failure to prevail in the lawsuit would foreclose other litigants from suing the call center was blatantly untrue and if true, would have negated our right to an appeal. Every case is decided on its own set of facts, and every judgment is subject to an appeal. Further, we were in state court, not before the U.S. Supreme Court on the threshold of a precedent-setting decision. Fear tactics dominated the moment, with authority figures (the few) in collusion against the powerless (the two of us, representing the multitudes who potentially had or would have to submit to their coercive strategies in the future).

The meeting appeared to be scripted in order to keep the case out of court and save face in the Reno Nevada community. Once again, clandestine homogeneity held sway— *like* treads the path with *like*——all in the name of keeping up appearances. The mighty assumed dominion over the perceived weakness of two individuals at the mercy of an unjust system.

To add insult to injury, the mediator told Kelly to go to a local children's hospital and "cuddle babies." She also analogized her family circumstances to ours, but comparisons had no place with us.

Finally, through duress, coercion, and a prevailing empathy deficit, we took the settlement offer (which discounted Kelly's lost earnings and was far less than the amount of the insurance policy, but that did not matter). We were exhausted and filled with a sense of loss, so when our lawyers invited us for drinks to "celebrate," we declined. All that we hoped to do was curl up in our hotel room and reflect on the debacle that had just occurred.

In the hotel lobby, Don conversed with Skip, expressing his disappointment in the outcome and his frustration at having to accept the settlement offer.

"Oh, that makes me feel really good," Skip said arrogantly.

Don got up and walked away angrily, accidentally leaving his room key card on a table. Unbeknownst to Don, Skip followed him, and as he caught up, he yelled out, "hey!"

As Don turned around, Skip flung the key card at him, and as Don bent down to retrieve it, Skip leaned over and asserted, "I'll bet you wish that my son were dead, too!" he said.

Don was horrified and felt sick to his stomach. "Oh, right! That's just what I'd want," he answered in an ironic tone, inflected with words that we cannot repeat here. Tears of anger and frustration flowed like a deluge, trapping us in another wave of grief—first, the loss of our son, then, our right to pursue justice in his name, while falling prey to the unprecedented egotism, narcissism, and self-created superiority of an oblivious few.

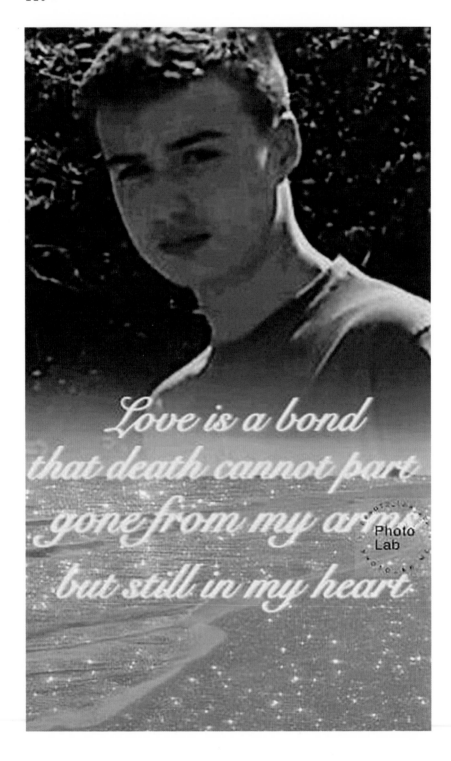

Love is a bond
that death cannot part
gone from my arms
but still in my heart

Photo
Lab

CHAPTER 13

THE POISONOUS STING OF CLANDESTINE HOMOGENEITY

When we returned to Florida, we felt completely helpless, like we were running in place, without a destination or purpose. Once again, we went through the mechanistic motions of daily living, not knowing where to turn next. Sleep was our only means of escape from the horrific realities of our 'new normal.' How could anything ever be the same again? Every breath was painful—physically and emotionally. At night, we lit candles for Dont'e, and in the bewitching hours of dawn, we sat in our kitchen, reliving events and circumstances as they occurred and could have been. These rituals continue to this day.

Our failed attempt at justice left us in a vacuous abyss with no way out. Despite our tumultuous childhoods, never once in our time on this planet did we contemplate ending our lives—until those moments in the early morning light.

Admittedly, feelings of purposelessness still surface—far too persistently—but we realize now that we have a mission to be our son's legacy and assume responsibility for lifting the veil of obscurity, indifference, and dismissiveness surrounding teen suicide.

While sitting quietly, we see our son—*everywhere*. Whether these sightings are grief hallucinations or holograms, it is difficult to say. In all events, our visions (such as that on page 107), an exact replica of Donté's forehead and eyebrows, were—and continue to be—very present in our world. Don found the image (right) one morning in the wee hours with a magnifying glass on our living room floor. We perceived it as a sign that, somehow, our son was 'coming through' from across the great divide, to tell us that he is still—and always will be—with us. Each time we see or feel a metaphysical presence, sign, or message, we know what it signifies. We do not require any justification, and parents who have lost children have had similar experiences.

These 'sightings' could also be a cry for justice in the name of those lost—a call for society to awaken to the endemic parasite of self-induced annihilation that takes hold of far too many promising, beautiful souls. They are not just statistics. They are precious lives that deserve to breathe freely in a world of diversity, acceptance, and universal love—the world in which our Dont'e lived until the last fifteen months of his life.

Our youth are increasingly subjected to the hateful din and oppression of white supremacy and the notion that they

do not matter. Authority figures stand by, most of the time inert—so caught up in the bureaucracy and mundane nature of their professions that they forget to serve people. Incredibly, the second lady who took Donté's call at the crisis call center said in mediation that no matter what anyone says or does, they (meaning our children) will take their own lives "anyway." Just another kid, just another life, drifting away. ***That's not okay.! It has to stop***.

The 'anyway' mindset equals destruction. Clandestine homogeneity is ubiquitous. It is like the air we breathe. In Donté's case, it inhered in the white supremacists at his high school, who plucked him from the herd like a sacrificial lamb, targeted, demoralized, and ultimately killed him with their 'otherness' ideology

As we write, we do not know—and we may never find out—whether our son died by his own hand, by the hand of another, or by facilitation—an act of omission— complicity through silence.

Although we have reached out to everyone in every possible stratum of society, we feel that our pleas (just like our son's) went unheeded. From the Bangor school administration to the local police department, from the Nevada state police to the district attorney and the state attorney general, from the Office of Civil Rights to the FBI controlling the entire northeastern region, to the Nevada Bar Association, Attorney General, and other entities, we found virtually no ally. Once again, these circumstances beg the pervasive question, "why?"

The deplorable acts and omissions of the Bangor Police Department and the funeral home in failing to preserve evidence, the turn-the-other-way tactics of school officials and students in the wake of Nazi propaganda that was allowed to exist in broad daylight, in the middle of the school's hallway, and the ensuing indifference, the call center's fatal mistake of no follow-up —not once, but twice—are not merely isolated incidents. Every omission is linked to another. Every omission, when viewed in the context of other events, is evidence of conspiratorial acts, and when those acts result in a death, a crime has been committed—an egregious wrong perpetrated against a family and humanity as a whole.

Then, there is the issue of our lawsuit, the attorneys' conduct, their lack of humanity in the face of our suffering, their failure to allow us, as parents, to be the architects of our case, and their indifference to our pleas for justice on the merits—or at least an attempt in furtherance of that objective. The final acts of inhumanity: an attack on our dignity and personhood, subjecting a grieving father to further emotional torture by undermining his request for a trial, the callous value judgments of the mediator, who preyed on a grieving mother's agony and vulnerability. CONSPIRACY and PREMEDITATION.

YET, WE RISE—in the name of Dont'e Izzo, in tribute to the marginalized—the George Floyds of the world who fall beneath the weight of an indifferent, murderous knee on their necks, for the fragile who succumb to the poisonous sting of clandestine homogeneity. Their voices may be silent, but their message resounds throughout the world and they will always be remembered. Human compassion will supplant indifference and self-induced annihilation!

With every breath, we will speak in the names of the fallen so that their pain will not be perpetuated. We will also take preemptive measures to stop the careless neglect of our children who cry out or endure inner pain and turmoil in silence. ***What do the words, "how can I help?" or "I care" cost anyone?*** Think about the inestimable value of a civil conversation, rather than hateful dialogue, memes, and actions that literally cause individuals to die.

We are committed to lifting our voices with those who, like us, have suffered the life-long tragedy of losing a child. Ignited with purpose, our spirits spark the flame of justice in unison with Kerri Countess, who lost her son Caleb to suicide in 2019—another precious life with a bright future—and we echo her mantra, "Suicide-free in 2023!" Visit forever14.org and join the crusade.

The "Forever 14" gentle warriors will join us as we begin our "Walk For Life" just after the publication of this book. Donald Izzo will be live-streamed, marching from Florida to Nevada. We move forward in Donté's name, we live through and with the agony. The words that have emanated from our souls represent our cry for justice.

AN OPEN LETTER TO PARENTS AND CHILDREN

From a Grieving Mother

Dear Parents and Children,

Having divulged the tragic story of how my son left the earth, I am still in a daze, with countless questions. As much as I cry out to God for answers, I may never truly know why. The bottom line is that I cannot turn back time, and I cannot get my son back, but I can and will be his voice. My husband and I are on a crusade to stop the suicide epidemic until the lifeblood no longer flows through our veins.

My son always knew that he could come to us, but the pressures of his world became a powder keg of destruction. Never in a million years did Don or I ever believe that our happy-go-lucky fifteen-year-old had thoughts of self-annihilation. Maybe, he took his life on the spur of the moment, in the throes of anguish, not knowing where to turn, or not seeing an alternative. Perhaps, he was edged on by peers, burdened by some hidden secret, living in a world of ideas and perspectives that were antithetical to his own—so much so, that he felt displaced. Possibly, maybe, perhaps ... No parent should have to go through these conjectures.

Life is precious, and the lives of our youth matter.

Death is finite, and there is no turning back.

Parents, I know that when you lose a child, you want to die. Life becomes devoid of purpose, and the what-ifs inundate your brain. Your heart ceases to beat, and you wonder why you're still here. Your faith is shaken, and every moment seems like an eternity.

Now is the moment to seize the day and articulate (No! Shout, if you feel the need!) all of your suppressed emotions. There are always people who care and who have the insight and compassion to listen—and to do something about the problem—whatever it is.

Children, the world needs you!

Social media icons and posts don't define who you are. They are entirely meaningless in your world. Your value comes not from the people who like or dislike you or those who admire your photos or make fun of you. They are not your judges and the dictators of your fate. YOU are the architect of your life and your destiny. CLAIM THEM AS RIGHTFULLY YOURS—NOW!

The opinions of others do not matter. What counts is **your life** *and that you wake up to the sunrise . . . and the next . . . and the next . . . for countless years to come, knowing that YOU ARE FAR MORE THAN ENOUGH!*

If you are a child or adolescent growing up in the twenty-first century, everything is not fine. The pressures of everyday life creep up on vulnerable minds and hearts and consume them from the inside-out. When it becomes all too much, you don't need an exit, but an outlet—someone to listen and to whom you can speak your mind. That person is your mother/father, school counselor, coach, best friend, confidante, mentor, or whomever you trust.

Our children remain silent because they cannot find the words. They forget that we adults were once children, too. They believe that we wouldn't understand. Worse, they think (like nearly everyone else in society) that suicide is a taboo subject. "Oh, you just don't talk about that," people say, hoping that the epidemic—more insidious than any contagion the world ever can experience—will, miraculously, go away. We hide away in our comfortable, oblivious little worlds, thinking that everything is rosy — until it is too late.

Unspoken words are weapons of mass destruction. Parents, sit down and talk to your children about suicide, speak openly and forthrightly on the subject and say something like, "if things ever get so tough that you have thoughts of suicide, you can come to me. I am here—your support system, your cheering section. Your life has infinite meaning, not only to me, but to the world. There is nothing that you cannot tell me or that I will not understand. You are safe here."

I recall telling the mother of a teen boy to approach him about suicide. She did so, and to her shock, she learned that her son had, in fact, contemplated it. That conversation saved his life!

If someone even mentions the word 'suicide' as an option, tell someone! Don't take that declaration lightly or wait for follow-through and regret your inaction!

YOU COULD SAVE SOMEONE FROM THE ULTIMATE IRREVERSIBLE ACT OF SELF-DESTRUCTION!

Every fourteen minutes, a child age ten to fifteen takes his or her own life. Your child does not have to fit a profile or pattern of behavior. Your child does not have to exhibit signs of clinical depression or have other mental or social conditions or spectrum disorders. Suicide is a silent killer. Red flags are not always visible.

The invisible parasite smolders within. Slowly and imperceptibly, children can shrink into a cocoon of their own insecurities and the lonely, dark abyss of their souls. One word, one look of disapproval, can set them off.

Conversely, one smile, one hug, one word of cautionary advice, and the courage to broach the topic of suicide can save a life and ensuing generations.

Educators and parents must unite in the common cause of demystifying the subject of suicide and join us in our crusade to save lives, educate, and inspire others to follow suit.

DARE TO GO WHERE OTHERS DO NOT WANT TO TREAD. SAVE CHILDREN FROM THE DARK NIGHT OF THEIR SOULS.

Parents, don't run, raise awareness. Don't cower, face the problem head-on. Speak as freely about suicide to children as you do about substance and alcohol abuse, as openly about self-worth as sex education, as candidly about the finality of suicide as the importance of self-hygiene. Think of innovative ways to broach the subject. Suggest that educators integrate the topic into the curriculum, have question-and-response forums, speak about the subject at home, have weekly sessions and "expression" groups.

Reach out to experts, guidance counselors, mental health professionals, and pay heed to their advice.

Be considerate. The formative years are the most stressful, so speak gently, intelligently— not over school PA systems!

Children, tell your friends not to be afraid of confiding if they entertain suicidal feelings or thoughts, and ask to do the same if you need them.

Approach your parents or other trusted mentors about your emotional state at any given moment—at all hours of the day and night.

FIND WAYS THROUGH, NOT WAYS OUT!

Most of all, be kind, say, "I love you," understand without judgment, communicate without fear or hesitation.

YOUR WORDS AND DEEDS CAN SAVE A LIFE AND FUTURE GENERATIONS!

In doing all of the above, you will pay homage to one of the universe's most beautiful souls, my son, the love of my life forever, Dont'e Izzo.

Thank you,

Kelly

IF ONLY YOU KNEW...

An Ode to Dont'e

Our Beloved Son, Dont'e,

We send this straight to heaven, standing near your shrine, where we light candles every night. We know that you can hear and see us.

What we would give to hear your laughter again, see you smile, joke around, and restore our faith in the world! Without you, the earthly plane is bereft of an angel who graced us for such a brief time—one who forever changed our life. If only you knew!

As our world painfully proceeds on its course, we make an effort to remember that now, God has you in his arms, and you make heaven an even more glorious place. All that we have lost now resides in a sphere outside and beyond our temporal vision, but it exists. It must! You are there!

You made us whole, you gave us life, and when you ceased to breathe, so did we. As hard as we try to go about our daily perambulations, everything seems meaningless without you. Our biggest question, 'why?' hangs over our heads and subsumes us in a bottomless pit. As we attempt to climb out, we reach for you, and somehow, we find you. We see you in every cloud formation, foliage, and flora. We perceive you in the light of each new day. Still—and forever—you will be that illumination for us. If only you knew!

We bemoan the fact that we cannot know your last thoughts or what brought you to that point. Why didn't you tell us? Were you scared? Did you think we would not understand? Was the tragic deed the fulfillment of a dare or something even more sinister? Did you know there was no turning back? Did you know we died, too?

Holidays, anniversaries and other commemorative events make our grief erupt like a volcano, and we struggle to find ourselves again. In truth, we never do. Every day is a reminder, and everything around us speaks your name— the wind, the birds, the summer storms that you used to watch with Dad.

We see your smiling face in the sunlight of a beautiful day, feel your tears in the rain. Dont'e! Everything is you!

We realize that you plunged into the depths of despair because the world as you knew and defined it ceased to exist. Hate and cruelty dictated your final act, turning you inexorably against yourself. Suddenly, after a short life of joy and pleasure, your bubble burst, and you were a boy without a purpose. But Dont'e, your life had supreme meaning! Everything beautiful that ever lived on Planet Earth manifested in your precious heart and acts of compassion. Your absence has left a void that never can be filled. If only you knew!

In your last moments, you did not know how much you were taking away—not only from your own life but generations that could have been here because of you. We will never see you walk down the aisle or bring children into the world —facsimiles of your worldview and ours and hope for a future that desperately needed all that you gave and had yet to bestow. If only you knew!

Despite your absence and the agony that has ensued, you are changing the world with your example and your story. You are raising awareness of the inequity of those who ignore or fail to speak out against the influences, transmitted on social media platforms, that cause our youth to lose perspective of what really matters: LIFE, NOT 'LIKES' AND OTHER SUPERFICIAL VALIDATION.

Your name, Dont'e Andrew Izzo, will forever be synonymous with healing wounds and raising awareness about the importance of interconnectedness—the "we," instead of the "me" mindset. If only you knew how much you live and have an influence! Or, perhaps, you do, for with every breath, you are with us and only a heartbeat away, You are the muse that has catalyzed the writing of this book and all that will follow. You have infused the words in our souls and the impetus to move forward—for and with you—for all time.

We miss you more than words can ever express!

With the greatest love that spans the universe and beyond, we invoke your memory, our life's foundation...

Forever,

Mom and Dad

DONTÉ'S MEMORY JOURNAL

Below, we share the comments of some of Donté's friends and family (Cousin Sara), who have kindly conceded to publishing their contributions, which were sent directly to Kelly.

Sara

When Donte and I were very young, my mom would always tell me some stories like when we were babies, he would be throwing toys at me while I would be watching tv and it didn't faze me. Another thing that I remember is that he wrote on one of my toy baby dolls in pen and was very up-set about it. When we were babies till about toddler age, we were close up until he moved to Maine with my aunt and uncle. Donte was always a sweet, loving person. I didn't really see him much growing up after growing out of the baby/toddler age, but from what I have seen on social me-dia and by his posts, and whenever my parents and I did hear anything from my aunt about how things were going, he was definitely happy growing up. Right before Donte passed, Donte and I were messaging a bit about how were doing, and I definitely didn't see this coming. I miss Donte every day and wish he never did what he did. It's hard in high school and I know from being in high school myself

with this generation. It's totally different from back then. Rest In Peace Dont'e.
—Your cousin Sara

Uncle Dan

One of my favorite memories is when I went to Maine and we were on the trampoline and I got in trouble for giving you peanut butter cups and soda. LOL!

Addy

I reminisce fondly about the days during the summer that we shared. Going to the fair and getting on that one ride as it started to downpour. Running back to your mother's car, hoping to dry off a little. I haven't enjoyed the fair that much since. Or our day at Black Beard's where I was too nervous to eat my pizza in front of you. I haven't gone back since. None of these places have the same light as they used to. I miss you so dearly and with my whole heart. I would do anything to go back and change our last conversation and have you know that I am sorry and that my world isn't the same without you in it.

Kenyan

Dont'e was one of my best friends and we did have a lot of good memories. One of my favorite memories was when Dont'e and I would make fun videos on your phone at your house. We both knew we weren't making the YouTube channel we planned on, but we still had a lot of fun making them. We had the same weird mind so we were always on board with each other's ideas.

Sam

I think one of the many good times I had with Donte was when Don bought us some fireworks and we put paintball masks on and shot Roman candles at each other.

Lauren

I'd love to tell you who I told [about Donté's posts], but it was so long ago I don't remember exactly who it was. I just knew people needed to know and attention should've been given. I have so many happy memories with Dont'e but one of my favorite and last memories with him was on a trip for leaders and we had stopped on the side of the river for lunch. He asked me if I wanted some Swedish fish and when he handed them to me, there was a little living fish mixed in with the Swedish fish. I screamed and dropped it all on the ground. He thought it was hilarious.

Derin

My best memories with Dont'e were when we used to draw together and he would draw Army guys for me and let me keep it. They were really cool and I still have them today

We used to joke around in math class and voice act together randomly.

And one of the best things was going paint balling with him. He got me to dive deeper into paint balling and he was quite profound when it came to paint balling, so I got inspired and started watching videos.

A Family Friend

Dear Dont'e:

You don't know me, but I have had the privilege of knowing you for some time. I have also come to know your extraordinary parents, who love you more than life itself. Through them, your spirit resonates so beautifully. I profoundly believe in and share your worldview, and I feel confident that through this book, their message and your legacy will be perpetuated. I can only imagine the depth and magnitude of courage that your parents had to summon to pay tribute to you in this fashion. I commend their physical, psychological, and emotional strength to lift their voices and beckon the forces of goodness and righteousness in your name.

May the better angels of humanity's nature prevail! You will live forever in my heart...A friend who loves you.

John and Mary Temporale (posted on Friday, March 10, 2017, on Dont'e tribute site)

I remember the first time we met.

"This is my son Dont'e," his dad said, brimming with pride.

He was an above-average boy with all of the American pressures piled upon him.

"What's in the bag?" I asked:

"It's for my pet, Stewie. He's a Chinese water dragon!

We talked for a while, and my wife and I could tell right off what a smart, polite young man he was.

Not like most people I knew—and certainly not like most other young people I have spoken with.

I love to engage our young in conversation. Dont'e and I bonded right away.

I chided him from time to time about his generation's music, their entertainment, and social media.

Dont'e could have given it right back to me like most of the youth I speak with: "You know, your generation ruined this, wrecked that, we have to pay for it . . ." and on-and on.

Not so with Dont'e.

Respect is what I would receive on any occasion we spoke.

He told me he wanted to pursue a military career—something I never hear from today's youth. I felt a deep respect growing in me for this young man and wished that if I had a son,I could do no better than Dont`e.

You see, God blessed me with a strong memory and it's at times like the present that I make the most of it.

I`ll miss this friend I knew for such a short time, but I`ll cherish my memories that I have of Dont`e forever.

Your friends,

John and Mary Temporale

UPDATE AND CONCLUSION

The Crusade Continues

(Don's Narrative)

It is inconceivable that two years have passed since I brought the inequities of the school department, the Bangor Police Department, the funeral home, and the medical examiner's office to light. I specifically requested a thorough investigation of the circumstances surrounding the post mortem handling of our son's effects, but I was not provided with any enlightenment as to why virtually no evidence was preserved. As mentioned earlier, the case was treated as 'just another suicide,' without empathy or regard to the circumstances surrounding Donté's death.

When I went to speak personally to Lieutenant Beaulieu of the Bangor Police Department, I provided a detailed account of what had occurred in the aftermath of Donté's passing. I emphasized that the evidence was discarded in violation of the police department, funeral home, and medical examiner's protocol—not to mention the flagrant disregard of our rights, as parents and next of kin, to retrieve those possessions.

When I asked Lieutenant Beaulieu whether he filed a report based on my investigations into our son's case, he replied, "this was a conversation, not an interview." This abnegation of responsibility is nothing less than careless indifference—and the powers that got away with it—while protecting the wrongdoers. *If it's not I, it doesn't concern me.* In that kind of world, how can any of us aspire to a higher quality of life?

Based on the information that I provided and the law as set forth in the Maine Criminal Code, Title 17-A, §204 (1), "A person is guilty of **aiding or soliciting** suicide if he intentionally aids or solicits another to commit suicide, and the other commits or attempts suicide" (emphasis added). Pursuant to §213 (1) of the same statute, "A person is guilty of **aggravated reckless conduct** if the person with terroristic intent engages in conduct that in fact creates a substantial risk of serious bodily injury to another person." Both are Class D offenses.

As a public servant, Lieutenant Beaulieu had a duty of care to recognize that Peter Blackwell's conduct fell within the purview of both sections of Maine's Criminal Code, and in failing to file a report, he breached his duty of care.

When I broached the subject with the U.S. Attorney General's office, I received the following reply from Brian MacMaster, Director of Investigations:

Dear Mr. Izzo:

There is nothing this office can do with regard to your concerns. Your son's death was investigated by the Bangor Police Department and if there is a basis for anyone to be charged with a crime, it would be the Bangor Police and the District Attorney's Office in Bangor to bring such charges.

Yet again, we received a 'passing-of-the-buck,' perfunctory response, without any expression of condolences. Accountability and compassion seem to be mere terms of art, and here we are, left without appropriate backup support.

My wife and I could rightfully have used any evidence that we obtained in pursuit of answers, most likely in furtherance of a criminal investigation. *Given that our son was the victim of white supremacist intimidation, we cannot rule out the possibility that he may not have died by his own hand or his compulsion to engage in self-annihilation was coerced—the tragic outcome of peer manipulation and treachery. The latter is probable, if not likely, given the circumstances surrounding his death.*

Our crusade is—and always will be— contemporaneous. So far, it has not yielded any answers whatsoever. Most recently, correspondence from the Bangor Police Department indicated that the cord (ligature) and a t-shirt were discarded, and other than photographs, the department has "no other items of evidence related to this case."

Subsequently, the Bangor Police Department's Chief of Police informed me that the lieutenant had no mandate to create or issue a written report, and while expressing condolences, he refused to pursue the matter further. Specifically, he stated that "we are done addressing this matter." Such an outright negation of my request was tantamount to closing the door in my face and sweeping the issue under the rug—yet another display of unmitigated indifference.

Just prior to the publication of this book, I received the following correspondence from the Office of the Chief Medical Examiner:

OFFICE OF CHIEF MEDICAL EXAMINER
STATE OF MAINE
37 State House Station
Augusta, ME 04333-0037

Mark Flomenbaum, MD, PhD
Chief Medical Examiner

ocme@maine.gov

Telephone: (207) 624-7180
Fax: (207) 624-7178

Lisa Funte, MD, PhD
Deputy Chief Medical Examiner

August 6, 2020

Donald Izzo
247 Burleigh Road
Bangor, ME 04401

By E-Mail Only: dpi04401@yahoo.com

Re: Evidence Inquiry

Dear Mr. Izzo,

I am writing to formally respond to your request for information on the Office of Chief Medical Examiner (OCME) policy and procedures regarding evidence obtained in death investigations.

It is our policy to bag, label, and release all evidentiary items back to the investigating law enforcement agency, as the OCME is not a physical evidence storage facility. If an article of clothing is contaminated with bodily fluids and considered a biohazard item, it will be discarded unless the investigating agency requests that it be retained. It would then be air-dried, bagged, and released to the investigating agency. Other clothing and personal belongings are bagged and released to the hired funeral home along with the remains.

During Dont'e's autopsy, a grey shirt and nylon ligature was present. The shirt was discarded as biohazard material as it was not identified by law enforcement as evidence. The ligature was discarded after permission was obtained from Sgt. Brock with Bangor Police Department. This permission was obtained during a phone call on March 7, 2017.

Please let me know if I can be of any further assistance.

Sincerely,

Lindsey Chasteen
Acting Office Administrator

The correspondence misstates the law and industry practices. As stated on page 71, protocol was not properly followed. Once evidentiary items are released to the investigating agency, that entity must preserve the evidence so that it can travel, with the decedent's remains, to the funeral home. The funeral home must then consult with the next of kin to determine whether or not to discard the decedent's personal effects. Donté's clothes, the ligature, and any other items found or taken from his person belonged to us and should have remained untouched until we gave the final word. Instead, our son's last earthly possessions were discarded outright, without our knowledge, consent, or explanation of the surrounding circumstances. Such conduct must not escape condemnation.

To think that every stratum of society turned its back on one innocent boy in failing to safeguard evidence is reprehensible. Our son is *every* child, and his suffering is everyone's plight who has ever experienced systemic alienation.

However that sinister objective was accomplished, words pulled that cord as much as physical acts of violence. Therefore, no matter how one views the circumstances, our son was a victim of a crime against humanity—one sacrificial life, without a voice.

I, Donald Izzo, may be but a speck within the Grand Scheme, challenging the titans of our society who purportedly serve the public, but I will not be defeated in our quest for justice. The bureaucratic wheel is not mightier than the human heart that beats in time with love—the greatest force of all.

Printed in Great Britain
by Amazon

48245701R00091